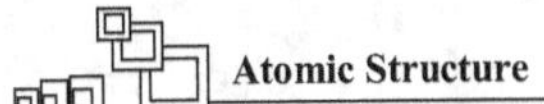

If the frequency is ν, it means that to travel ν waves, it takes one second, then to travel one wavelength, the time taken is:

No. of wavelength	Time
$\nu\lambda$	1s
λ	$\dfrac{\lambda \times 1s}{\nu\lambda} = \dfrac{1}{\nu}$ s.

$$\therefore T = \frac{1}{\nu}$$

So, it follows that

$$c = \frac{\lambda}{T} = \lambda \times \nu$$

The velocity 'c' of all types of electromagnetic radiations including light is established experimentally. It is a constant in vacuum, equal to 3×10^8 ms^{-1}. Since all electromagnetic radiations travel with the same velocity, they differ from are another in their wavelengths and consequently their frequencies.

WAVE NATURE	λ in Å	
Radio waves	$3 \times 10^7 - 3 \times 10^{14}$	
Infrared (IR)	$7600 - 3 \times 10^7$	Wavelength decreases
Visible	$3800 - 7600$	Frequency increases
Ultraviolet (UV)	$1 - 3800$	Energy increases
X–rays	$10^{-2} - 10$	
γ–rays	10^{-4} to 10^{-1}	

(b) **Atomic Spectra:** When white light is passed through a prism, it is separated into light of seven colours (VIBGYOR) or radiations of different wavelengths. The pattern obtained by splitting or sorting out of radiations into its component wavelengths is called a spectrum. The spectrum of white light when analyzed by spectrometer (an instrument that indicates the wavelengths/frequencies of individual components of a radiation) is a continuous spectrum, suggesting that white light is made up of all possible wavelengths or frequencies of radiations. If a gas is heated, it emits light. When this emitted light is analysed in a spectrometer, the spectra obtained consists of a series of well–defined sharp lines, each line corresponding to a definite wavelength or frequency. These line spectra are characteristic of atoms.

In spectroscopic work, a term called wave number is often used. It is defined as the number of wavelengths per cm. It is given as:

$$\text{Wave number} = \bar{\nu} = \frac{1}{\lambda}$$

Since $\quad c = \nu \times \lambda$

$$\bar{\nu} = \frac{\nu}{c}$$

Spectral lines are associated with electronic transitions. Hydrogen atom contains only one electron and the spectrum is the simplest to analyze. The spectrum of atomic hydrogen consists of a number of discrete lines in the UV, visible and I.R regions. Each line corresponds to a particular frequency or wavelength. The space between two lines represents the frequency range in which no radiation is emitted by the hydrogen atom. Lines observed in the atomic spectra of hydrogen are grouped into the several series called spectral series. A group of lines appearing in the UV region is called the Lyman series; that in the visible region is called Balmer series; in the I. R region there are three – Paschen, Brackett and Pfund series.

The wave number of any line of hydrogen atom can be represented as a difference of two terms by the formula.

$$\bar{\nu} = R\left[\frac{1}{n_1^2} - \frac{1}{n_2^2}\right]$$

where R is called Rydberg constant (as this was formulated by Rydberg) and n_1 and n_2 are integers $(n_2 > n_1, n_1 > 0)$.

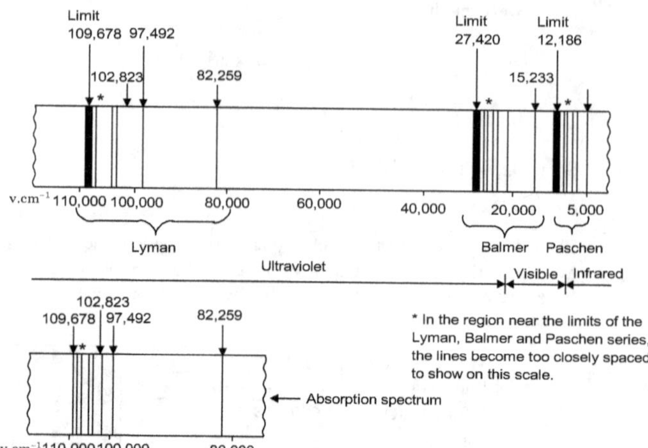

(C) **Quantum Theory:** According to this theory, a body cannot emit or absorb energy in the form of radiation of continuous energy; energy can be taken up or given out as whole number multiples of a definite amount known as a quantum. Light is imagined to consist of a stream of particles called photons. It E is the energy of a photon; its quantum for a particular radiation of frequency $v\ sec^{-1}$ is given by quantum theory as

$$E = hv$$

where h is a universal constant known as planck's constant; $h = 6.626 \times 10^{-27}$ erg second or 6.626×10^{-34} Joule second (Js).

$$E = hv = \frac{hc}{\lambda} = hc\ \bar{v}$$

According to quantum theory, a body can emit or absorbs either one quantum of energy (hv) or whole number multiples of this unit, 2hv, 3hv.........nhv.

THE BOHR'S MODEL:

In 1913 more than a decade before quantum mechanics was established, the Danish physicist Niels Bohr proposed a model of the hydrogen atom based on a linear hybrid combination of classical and early quantum physics. Although a fully developed quantum model later replaced Bohr's model, it nevertheless served as a powerful stimulus of later developments.

Bohr retained the Rutherford model of a central positively charged nucleus containing practically all the mass surrounded by a planetary system of electrons whose number is equal to the protons. He made use of Planck's quantum theory and gave the following postulates.

In any atom electrons can rotate only in certain selected (or permissible orbits without radiating energy). Such orbits are known as stable or non-radiating orbits or stationary states. These orbits are circular with well–defined radii. These orbits are numbered 1, 2, 3,.....(from the nucleus). Orbits are paths of revolution of electrons. A spherical surface around the nucleus, which contains orbits of equal energy and radius, is called a shell. The shells are denoted as K, L, M, N, ...

Each stationary state or (orbit) corresponds to a certain energy level (i.e., as long as the electron is in the particular stationary state it has a definite amount of energy).
The energy associated with an electron is least in the K shell and it increases as we pass to L, M, N, ... shells.

An electron can jump from one stationary state to another. For an electron to jump from an inner orbit of energy E_1 to an outer orbit of energy E_2, it should absorb the equivalent of a quantum of energy = $E_2 - E_1 = hv$, when v is the frequency of radiation absorbed. Similarly, when it jumps back from the outer to the inner orbit, it will emit an equal amount of energy in the form of radiation.

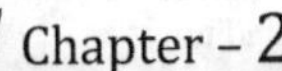

Chapter – 2

India's First Trick Based Study Material

ATOMIC STRUCTURE

1 ATOMIC MODELS

1.1 THE PARTICLES OF MATTER & ATOMIC MODELS

In 1807, an English school teacher, John Dalton gave the first convincing argument about the existence of atoms. He relied upon a large number of experiments and measurements to measure the masses of elements that combined together, and assembled arguments that strangely indicated the existence of atoms. Dalton picturised atoms as featureless spheres like billiard balls. Today we know that atoms have an internal structure and are built from even smaller particles. It is this knowledge that provides an insight into the difference between elements.

1.2. MODEL 1–THE PLUM PUDDING MODEL

The earliest experimental evidence of the existence of sub–atomic particles was the discovery in 1807 by the British physicist J.J. Thompson. He was investigating "cathode rays", He said that cathode rays are emitted when a high potential difference (a high voltage) is applied between two electrodes in an evacuated glass tube. Thompson showed that cathode rays are streams of negatively charged particles. They came from inside the atoms that made up the electrode called cathode. Thomson found that the charged particles were the same regardless of the metal he used for the cathode. These particles were named electrons and denoted e^-. Later the mass of the electrons was experimentally calculated by Robert Milkan as 9.1×10^{-28} g. Goldstein discovered the existence of protons, (positively charged particles) and neutrons (neutral charged particles) was discovered by Chadwick.

Table 1:
Properties of Electrons, Protons & Neutrons

		ELECTRON (e)	PROTON (p)	NEUTRON (n)
MASS	AMU	0.000549	1.00727	1.00866
	GRAMS	9.11×10^{-28}	1.675×10^{-24}	1.675×10^{-24}
	RELATIVE	$\dfrac{1}{1837}$	1	1
CHARGE	COULOMBS	-1.602×10^{-19}	$+ 1.602 \times 10^{-19}$	Zero
	ESU	$- 4.8 \times 10^{-10}$	$+ 4.8 \times 10^{-10}$	Zero
	RELATIVE	-1	$+1$	Zero

Based on these discoveries J.J. Thompson proposed the plum pudding model. This model proposed that atoms are blobs of a positively charged jellylike material, with electrons suspended in it like raisins in a pudding.

1.3 MODEL 2–THE RUTHERFORD MODEL

In 1908, the plum pudding model was overthrown by a simple experiment.

The New Zealander Ernest Rutherford asked two students to shoot α-particles (he knew that some element like Radon emit positively charged particles, which he called alpha (α) particles) toward a piece of gold foil only a few atoms thick. If atoms were indeed like blobs of positively charged jelly, then all the α–particles would leave similar paths as they move through the foil.

What his students observed astonished everyone around them. Although almost all the α–particles did pass through, about 1 in 20,000 was deflected through more than 90°, and a few α–particles bounced straight back in the direction from which they had came. "It was almost incredible," said Rutherford, "as if you had fired a 15-inch shell at a piece of tissue paper and it can back and hit you".

The explanation was that atoms had to contain massive point like centers of positively charge surrounded by a large volume of mostly empty space. Rutherford called the point of positively charged region, the nucleus. He reasoned that closer the path of the α–particles to the nucleus of the atom, greater the deflection it experiences and the α–particles which directly hit on the molecules would rebound back.

The electrons are thinly distributed throughout the space around the nucleus. If the nucleus in a hydrogen atom were the size of a fly at the center of a cricket stadium, then the space occupied by the electron would be about the size of the entire cricket stadium.

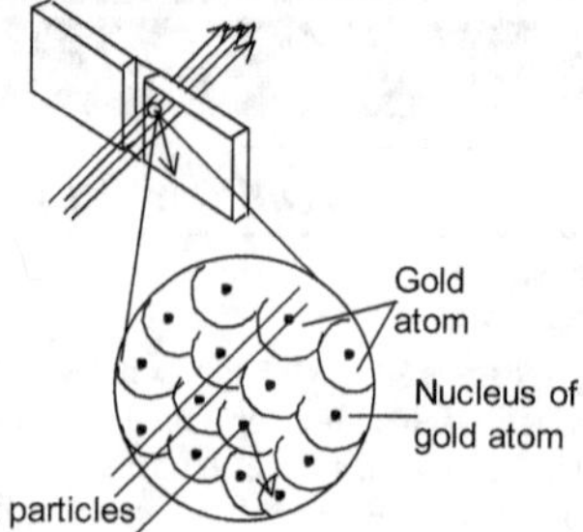

In an atom the positive charge of the nucleus exactly cancels the negative charge of the surrounding electrons. So, for each electron outside the nucleus, there must be a matching positively charged particle inside the nucleus called the proton.

Since electrons would be attracted by the nucleus and would eventually fall into it, Rutherford assumed that electron were not stationary and that they move in a circular path around the nucleus using the electrostatic force of attraction. This was analogues to the earth moving around the sun using the gravitational force of attraction.

1.4 MODEL 3: THE BOHR'S MODEL:

As a prelude to Bohr's theory, we should have an introduction to (i) nature of radiations (ii) atomic spectra and (iii) quantum theory.

(a) Radiations: Ordinary light, X–rays, γ–rays etc. are called electromagnetic radiations and they have wave characteristics. These radiations are called electromagnetic because when they pass through a point in space, they produce oscillating electric and magnetic fields at that point. In 1873 a Scottish physicist, James Clark Maxwell showed that a static charge or a charge with uniform velocity sets up an electric and magnetic fields which gives rise to an energy density in space associated with the electric and magnetic fields, but the energy density remains constant. On the other hand, if we were to change the velocity of the charged particle, the energy density varies and then gives rise to electromagnetic waves.

There are three fundamental characteristics associated with wave motion. They are (i) wavelength (λ) (ii) frequency (ν) and (iii) velocity (c).

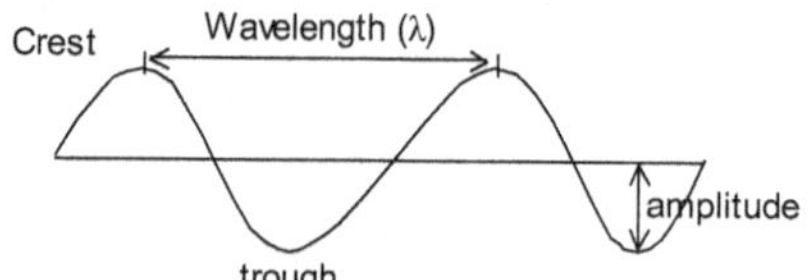

(i) Wavelength: Consider a wave profile as shown in the above figure. The distance between two successive crests or troughs is known as wavelength (λ). It is measured in cm or Angstrom unit (Å)

$1Å = 10^{-8}$ cm $= 10^{-10}$ m

Some times nanometer, ($1nm = 10^{-9}$ m) is also used.

(ii) Frequency: The number of waves that pass through a given point in one second is called its frequency (no. of waves per sec.). Frequency (ν) is expressed in cycles per sec (cps) or Hertz (Hz).

(iii) The distance traveled by a wave in one second is its velocity.

$$\text{velocity} = \frac{\text{wavelength}}{T} = \frac{\text{Distance travelled in a wavelength}}{\text{Time taken to travel one wavelength}}$$

When an electron absorbs energy, it passes from an inner to an outer orbit; then the electron or the atom is said to be in an excited state. An exited electron has always to fall back to a lower orbit within a very short interval or time and as it does so, it releases the quantum of energy absorbed during excitation.

Unlike in Rutherford's model where an electron should constantly emit radiations (Maxwell's theory) since it gets accelerated while moving around the nucleus (with constant speed but varying direction), in Bohr's model all orbits are stable–the electron would not be radiating energy. This is because the angular momentum of an electron moving in a stable state is quantized. The angular momentum of an electron moving in a circular orbit is mvr, where m is the mass, v is the velocity and r is the radius of the orbit. According to Bohr, angular momentum is given by

$$mvr = n\hbar$$

$$\text{Where } \hbar = \frac{h}{2\pi}$$

$$\therefore mvr = \frac{nh}{2\pi}$$

where n is a positive integer 1, 2, 3, …. and is known as a Quantum number. The angular momentum can, therefore, be $\dfrac{h}{2\pi}, \dfrac{2h}{2\pi}, \dfrac{3h}{2\pi}, \ldots\ldots\ldots \dfrac{nh}{2\pi}$.

This principle is known as quantization of angular momentum.

These postulates of Bohr lead us to:

(i) Explain the permanence of the atom. Since electron neither loses energy nor gains energy as long as it is in its ground state, there is no question of the electron falling into the nucleus and so Bohr's theory accounts for the permanence of the atom.

(ii) Using these postulates, Bohr calculated the energy of the electron in an orbit. In a hydrogen atom, the electron revolves around the nucleus in a circular orbit. For the system to be stable, the coulombic attraction between the electron and the nucleus must be the source of the necessary centripetal force for circular motion. i,e. coulombic force of attraction = centripetal force

$$\frac{K \times (Ze) \times e}{r^2} = \frac{mv^2}{r}$$

where,

- e = magnitude of charge on an electron (or a proton).
- Z = atomic number (e.g. for H–atom, Z = 1)
- r = radius of the orbit
- m = mass of the electron
- v = velocity of the electron
- K = coulomb's law constant $= \dfrac{1}{4\pi\varepsilon_\circ}$

$$= 9 \times 10^9 \frac{Nm^2}{C^2} \text{ in SI system and} = 1 \text{ in CGS units.}$$

The above equation becomes,

$$\frac{K.Ze^2}{r} = mv^2 \qquad\qquad \ldots\ldots\ldots(i)$$

The angular momentum of a body moving in a circular orbit is mvr and as per the Bohr's theory,

$$mvr = \frac{nh}{2\pi}$$

$$\therefore v = \frac{nh}{2\pi mr}$$

Substituting in equation (i)

$$\frac{Kze^2}{r} = m\left(\frac{nh}{2\pi mr}\right)^2 \qquad\qquad \ldots\ldots\ldots(ii)$$

Solving for r, we get

$$r = \frac{n^2 h^2}{4\pi^2 K Z m e^2} \qquad \ldots\ldots\ldots(iii)$$

This is the equation for the radius of the orbit of the electron. For hydrogen atom in the ground state, $n = 1$ and substituting the values of the constants in equation (iii), we get

$r_1 = 0.529 \times 10^{-10}$ m $= 0.529$ Å

The radius of any other orbit in H atoms will be,

$r_n = 0.529\ n^2$ Å

The total energy of the electron will be the sum of the potential and kinetic energies.

Total energy, $E = PE + KE$

The potential energy is the energy due to coulombic attraction and so

$$PE = \frac{-KZe^2}{r}$$

Kinetic energy can be calculated from the velocity of the electron.

$$KE = \frac{1}{2}mv^2$$

$$\text{Total energy, } E = \frac{-KZe^2}{r} + \frac{1}{2}mv^2 \qquad \ldots\ldots\ldots(iv)$$

Substituting the value of mv^2 from the equation (i),

$$E = \frac{-KZe^2}{r} + \frac{KZe^2}{2r} \qquad \ldots\ldots\ldots(v)$$

$$E = \frac{-KZe^2}{2r} \qquad \ldots\ldots\ldots(vi)$$

Substituting (iii) in (vi), we get

$$E = \frac{-2\pi^2 K^2 Z^2 m e^4}{n^2 h^2} \qquad \ldots\ldots\ldots(vii)$$

From equation (v), it can seen that the magnitude of the potential energy is twice that of kinetic energy.

The negative sign in the equation (vii) represents that the energy is released when the electron moves from ∞ to any orbit. Thus the energy of the electron in an atom is lower than the energy of a free electron (which is zero). As 'r' increases, the energy becomes less negative which means that energy increases.

We can calculate the energy of the ground state of the electron in hydrogen atom.

$$E = \frac{-2 \times (3.14)^2 \times \left(9 \times 10^9\right) \times 1^2 \times 9.1 \times 10^{-31} \times \left(1.6 \times 10^{-19}\right)^4}{1^2 \times 6.626 \times 10^{-34}}$$

$E = -2.179 \times 10^{-18}$ J per atom

$E = -13.6$ eV per atom ($\because$ 1eV $= 96.368$ J/mole)

$E = -1312$ kJ/mole

From this ground state energy of hydrogen atom, we can find the energy in any other atom.

$$E_n = E_H \times \frac{Z^2}{n^2}$$

n can have only positive integral values and so the total energy of the electron is quantized.

Suppose an electron jumps from n_2 to n_1 level in a hydrogen atom ($n_2 > n_1$)

$$E_{n_1} = \frac{-2\pi^2 k^2 m e^4}{n_1^2 h^2} \quad \text{(in C.G.S. units)};$$

$$E_{n_2} = \frac{-2\pi^2 k^2 m e^4}{n_2^2 h^2}$$

The difference in energy emitted is

$$h\nu = \frac{-2\pi^2 k^2 m e^4}{h^2}\left[\frac{1}{n_2^2} - \frac{1}{n_1^2}\right]$$

$$\nu = \frac{2\pi^2 k^2 m e^4}{h^3}\left[\frac{1}{n_1^2} - \frac{1}{n_2^2}\right]$$

$$\bar{\nu} = \frac{\nu}{c} = \frac{2\pi^2 k^2 m e^4}{h^3 c}\left[\frac{1}{n_1^2} - \frac{1}{n_2^2}\right]$$

$$\bar{\nu} = R\left[\frac{1}{n_1^2} - \frac{1}{n_2^2}\right]$$

$$R = \frac{2\pi^2 k^2 m e^4}{h^3 c} = 109737 \text{ cm}^{-1}$$

This empirical value of R deduced from Balmer, Lyman and other series agreed excellently with the experimental results. This is the triumph for Bohr's theory. From the foregoing discussion, we can understand that Bohr's theory has given an expression for the energy of the electron of hydrogen atom in the nth orbit as

$$E_n = \frac{-21.76 \times 10^{-19} \text{ J}}{n^2}$$

$$E_n = \frac{-13.6}{n^2}\text{ eV}$$

It can be assumed that the electron and the nucleus revolve around their common center of mass. Therefore, instead of the mass of the electron, the reduced mass of the system was introduced and the equation becomes

$$\bar{\nu} = \frac{2\pi^2 k^2 \mu e^4}{h^3 c}\left[\frac{1}{n_1^2} - \frac{1}{n_2^2}\right]$$

where μ is the reduced mass $= \dfrac{Mm}{M+m}$, whose M is the mass of the nucleus and m is the mass of the electron.

INTERPRETATION OF SPECTRAL SERIES

The hydrogen atom contains only one electron in first orbit (K shell). This is the normal orbit or ground state and represents the stationary state of the unexcited atom. Energy may be absorbed by this electron, which is then raised from its normal orbit to a higher energy level. In this new level, the electron possesses more energy and is less stable than before. It will, therefore, fall towards the nucleus until it reaches either the normal orbit or some intermediate level. In this process, energy is released as a photon of frequency E = hv.

Spectral lines are produced by radiation of photons and the position of the lines on the spectrum is determined by the frequency of photons emitted. Transition to innermost level (n= 1) from higher levels (n = 2, 3, 4 etc.) gives the first, second, third etc., line of the Lyman series. The general idea will be clear by a study of the following figure.

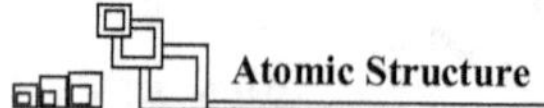

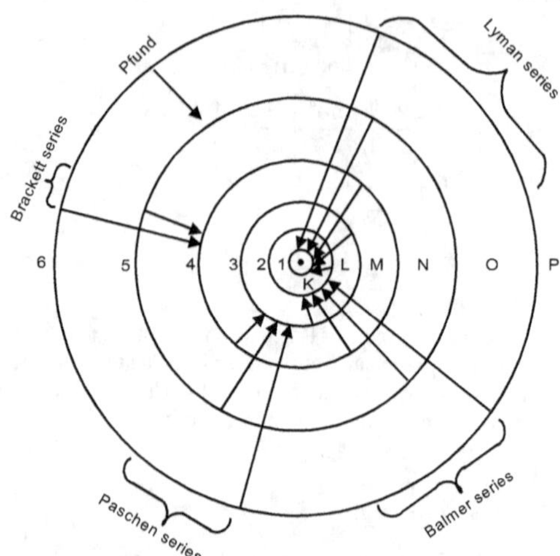

which shows the various energy changes leading to various lines in the spectrum. Thus Bohr's theory is able to account for the observed spectral lines and series in detail and with accuracy for the hydrogen atom.

Hydrogen atom contains only one electron but its spectrum consists of several lines. Why? A sample of hydrogen contains a very large number of atoms. When energy is supplied, the electrons present in different atoms may be excited to different energy level. These electrons when they fall back to various lower levels emit radiations of different frequencies. Each electronic transition produces a spectral line. Energy is absorbed by an atom when an electron moves from the inner energy level to the outer energy level. The amount of energy necessary to remove an electron from its lowest level ($n = 1$) to infinite distance resulting in the formation of a free ion is called the ionization potential. The ionization energy of hydrogen is 2.18×10^{-18} J or 13.595 electron – volts ($1\ eV = 1.602 \times 10^{-19}$ J).

If an electron acquires more than enough energy to permit its removal from the atom, the extra energy is carried off by the free electron as kinetic energy. Because of the very small magnitude of the quanta of translational (i.e. kinetic) energy, this energy is essentially continuously variable. The spectrum beyond the series limit thus appears continuous; from the position of continuum, we may calculate the ionization potential.

DEFECTS:

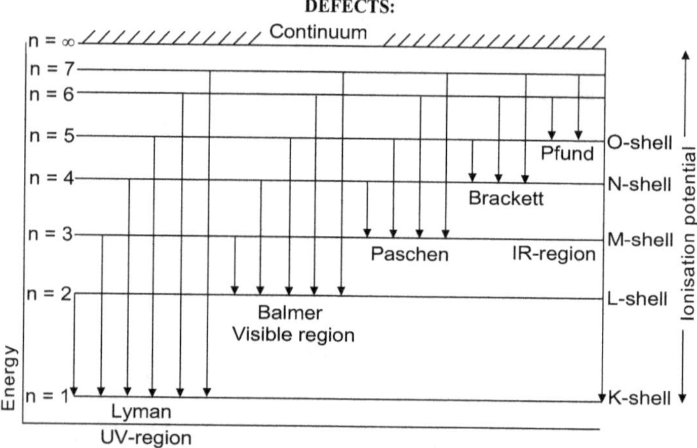

Bohr's model was quite successful in accounting for the main features of the hydrogen spectrum and also the spectrum of He^+ ion (which has only one electron). However, it failed to predict the energy states of more complicated atoms. It is applicable only for one electron system because it does not take into account inter–electronic repulsions.

Even in the case of hydrogen atom, the spectral lines under high resolution showed fine structure (a number of closely packed lines), which is not explained by Bohr's theory.

Bohr's theory could not explain why an electron does not get excited if it is provided energy that will allow it to exist in between two energy levels.

Illustration 1

Question: The energies of the electron in the second and third orbits of the hydrogen atom are -5.42×10^{-12} and -2.41×10^{-12} ergs respectively. Calculate the wavelength of the emitted radiation when the electron drops from the third to the second orbit.

Solution: The emitted radiation will have energy equal to the energy difference between the third and the second orbit.

$$\Delta E = E_3 - E_2$$
$$= -2.41 \times 10^{-12} - (-5.42 \times 10^{-12})$$
$$= 3.01 \times 10^{-12} \text{ ergs.}$$
$$1 \text{ erg} = 10^{-7} \text{ J}$$
$$\therefore \Delta E = 3.01 \times 10^{-19} \text{ J}$$

This energy of radiation corresponds to a wavelength of

$$\Delta E = h\nu = \frac{hc}{\lambda}$$

$$\lambda = \frac{hc}{\Delta E} = \frac{6.626 \times 10^{-34} \times 3 \times 10^8}{3.01 \times 10^{-19}}$$
$$= 6.6039 \times 10^{-7} \text{ m}$$
$$= 6603.9 \times 10^{-10} \text{ m}$$
$$= \mathbf{6603.9 \text{ Å}}$$

Illustration 2

Question: Calculate the wavelength in Å of the photon that is emitted when an electron in the Bohr orbit $n = 2$ returns to the orbit $n = 1$ in the hydrogen atom. The ionization potential of the ground state of the hydrogen atom is 2.17×10^{-11} erg per atom.

Solution: Energy of nth level in the hydrogen is inversely proportional to n^2.

$$E_n \propto \frac{1}{n^2}$$

$$E_n = \frac{-2.17 \times 10^{-11}}{n^2}$$

When electron falls from $n = 2$ to $n = 1$ the energy emitted would be,

$$E_1 = \frac{-2.17 \times 10^{-11}}{1^2}$$

$$E_2 = \frac{-2.17 \times 10^{-11}}{2^2}$$

$$\Delta E = E_2 - E_1 = 2.17 \times 10^{-11}\left[1 - \frac{1}{2^2}\right]$$

$$= 2.17 \times 10^{-11} \times \frac{3}{4} \text{ erg /atom} = 2.17 \times 10^{-18} \times \frac{3}{4} \text{ J/atom}$$

$$\Delta E = \frac{hc}{\lambda}$$

$$\lambda = \frac{hc}{\Delta E} = \frac{6.626 \times 10^{-34} \times 3 \times 10^8}{2.17 \times 10^{-18} \times \frac{3}{4}} = 1.22138 \times 10^{-7} \text{ m}$$

$$\lambda = \mathbf{1221.38 \text{ Å}}$$

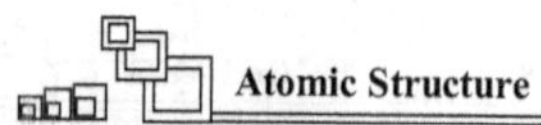

Illustration 3

Question: The electron energy in hydrogen atom is given by $E = \dfrac{-21.7 \times 10^{-12}}{n^2}$ ergs. Calculate the energy required to remove an electron completely from n = 2 orbit. What is the longest wavelength (in cm) of light that can be used to cause this transition?

Solution:

$$E_n = \frac{-21.7 \times 10^{-12}}{n^2} \text{ ergs}$$

$$E_2 = \frac{-21.7 \times 10^{-12}}{2^2}$$

Removing the electron completely from the atom implies that the electron has been exited to the level ∞.

$$\therefore \; E_\infty = \frac{-21.7 \times 10^{-12}}{\infty^2} = 0$$

$$\Delta E = E_\infty - E_2 = \frac{21.7 \times 10^{-12}}{4} \text{ ergs}$$

$$\Delta E = \frac{21.7 \times 10^{-12}}{4} \times 10^{-7} \text{ Joule} = \mathbf{5.425 \times 10^{-19}\ J}$$

$$\Delta E = \frac{hc}{\lambda}$$

$$\therefore \; \lambda = \frac{hc}{\Delta E} = \frac{6.626 \times 10^{-34} \times 3 \times 10^8}{5.425 \times 10^{-19}} = 3.66414 \times 10^{-7} \text{ m.}$$

$$\therefore \; \lambda = \mathbf{3664.14\ \mathring{A}}$$

Illustration 4

Question: There is one hydrogen atom in the ground state. It is excited to a higher energy level n. When the electron comes back to the ground state, it emits radiation. What is the maximum number of unique wavelengths it can emit?

Solution:

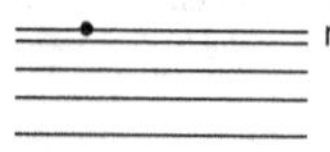

Let us imagine the electron to be in the energy level n. When it comes to the ground state it can come in many number of ways. Either it will directly come to n = 1, in which case it will emit only one wavelength (corresponding to n to 1) or it can fall to n =2 and then from n = 2 to n = 1, in which case it will emit two unique wavelengths (one corresponding to n to 2 and the other corresponding to n = 2 to n = 1) and so on. We have to find how the electron must come back by emitting maximum number of unique wavelengths. It is very clear that every jump of the electron would radiate a unique wavelength as

$$\frac{1}{\lambda} = R\left[\frac{1}{n_1^2} - \frac{1}{n_2^2}\right]$$

λ cannot be same for different sets of n_1 and n_2.

The only way maximum wavelengths can be emitted is when the electron comes back to ground state by maximum jumps. This means the electron must jump stepwise i.e., n to n − 1 to n − 2 to n −3 and so on. This means the total jumps would be n − 1 and so would be the number of unique wavelength.

$$\therefore \; \mathbf{n - 1}$$

PROFICIENCY TEST– I

The following 10 questions deal with the basic concepts of this section. Answer the following briefly. Go to the next section only if your score is greater than or equal to 8.
Do not consult the study material while attempting the questions.

1. Rutherford's model suggests that the central part of the atom contains _________ charged particles.

2. According to Bohr's theory the electron will not emit radiation in those orbits where the angular momentum is _________.

3. (True/False): When an electron in the ground state of a hydrogen atom is excited with an energy that is greater than $E_2 - E_1$ but less than $E_3 - E_1$ the electron will get excited to n = 2.

4. (True/False): If the wavelength of a transition is specified, then the energy level involved in the transition can be identified, as each transition is associated with a unique wavelength.

5. According to planck's quantum theory, $E =$ _________.

6. Energy of an electron in the nth level is = _________ eV.

7. In the Bohr's orbit of hydrogen atom the magnitude of potential energy of an electron is _________ × kinetic energy.

8. The ionisation energy of hydrogen atom is _________ eV.

9. An electron is in n = 4 in a hydrogen atom sample. If the electron is allowed to reach n = 1 in all possible way in the atoms then the maximum number of unique wavelengths the sample would emit is _________.

10. (True/False): The radius of the nth orbit in a hydrogen atom is directly proportional to n^2.

ANSWERS TO PROFICIENCY TEST– I

1. positively

2. integral multiple of $\dfrac{h}{2\pi}$ or $\dfrac{nh}{2\pi}$

3. False. The electron would not be excited at all.

4. True

5. $h\nu$

6. $\dfrac{-13.6\, Z^2}{n^2}$

7. 2

8. 13.6

9. 6

10. True, $r \propto n^2$

2 DUAL NATURE OF MATTER

2.1 DE BROGLIE WAVELENGTH

Nature abounds in symmetries of all kinds. If light can be both wave and particle, is it possible that matter can also have these properties? Can the electron, traditionally regarded as a particle since its discovery in 1898, also have a wave aspect? More specifically, can we assign a wavelength and a frequency to a moving electron?

In 1924, the French physicist Prince Louis–Victure Broglie, motivated entirely by this symmetry argument, answered yes to these questions. He proposed that an electron of energy E and linear momentum 'p' could be defined by a matter wave whose wavelength and frequency are given by

$$\lambda = \frac{h}{p} \quad ; \quad v = \frac{E}{h}$$

in which h is the Planck's constant. The wavelength of a moving particle calculated above is called its de Broglie wavelength. De Broglie shared the 1929 Nobel prize for his discovery of the wave nature of matter.

Objects such as marbles or cricket balls do not seem at all wave like. We can understand why this is so because the Planck's constant h is so small and the momentum p of even slowly moving macroscopic particles is so large that the calculated de Broglie wavelengths of such objects are small indeed, being many orders of magnitude smaller than the size of an atomic nucleus.

2.2 HEISENBERG'S UNCERTAINITY PRINCIPLE

First derived by the German physicist Werner Heisenberg, it states that. It is not possible to measure, simultaneously, the position and the momentum of a particle with unlimited precision.

If Δx is the uncertainty in position and Δp is uncertainty in momentum then,

$$\Delta x \times \Delta p \geq \frac{h}{4\pi}$$

The message of the uncertainty principle is that there is a limit to the extent to which the concept of "particle" can be extended from the Newtonian world to the quantum world. In the quantum world, it is wrong to imagine that a particle really has a definite position and momentum but, for some reason, we are not able to measure it. It is wrong to visualize a particle as a tiny mass point moving along a path, with its position and velocity well defined at every instant. The very notion of "trajectory" belongs to the Newtonian world, not to the quantum world.

3 THE QUANTUM MODEL

Improving on the Bohr Model, Sommerfield, in order to account for the additional lines present in the spectra of atoms, assumed that each principal energy level contains a number of sub–levels, each of which possesses slightly different energy. The subsidiary orbits are designated s, p, d and f (these letters standing for the nature – sharp, principal, diffuse and fundamental – of the lines in the spectra). The number of sub–levels in any particular energy level is fixed. The various sub–levels in K, L, M, N etc., shells and the maximum number of electrons that may be present in each of them are given below:

Shell	K	L		M			N			
Sublevels	1s	2s	2p	3s	3p	3d	4s	4p	4d	4f
Max. no. of electrons	2	2	6	2	6	10	2	6	10	14

The principle quantum number, n can have values 1, 2, 3, ..., and is indicative of the major energy levels of the electron in an atom in a gross way. This is similar to the quantum levels in Bohr's theory. The azimuthal quantum number, l, has values from 0 to (n–1), for each value of n. It is a measure of the angular momentum of the electron, which is $\frac{h}{2\pi}\sqrt{l(l+1)}$ in magnitude. Values of $l = 0, 1, 2, 3, ...,$ are designated by the letters s, p, d, f ..... The magnetic quantum number m is indicative of the component of the angular momentum vector in any one chosen direction, usually the z–axis. The values of m are from $-l$ to $+l$ including zero for any value of l. An electron can spin either in clockwise direction or in anticlockwise direction. Spin quantum number, 's' can have two values $+\frac{1}{2}$ and $-\frac{1}{2}$ and also represented by arrow pointing in opposite direction i.e. ↑ and ↓ for any particular value of magnetic quantum number.

Permissible values of the quantum numbers for various orbitals are mentioned in the table given on next page.

Table: Permissible values of quantum numbers for atomic orbital

Pr. Q. no. 'n'	Azimuthal Quantum no. '*l*'	Magnetic Quantum no. 'm'	Spin Quantum no. 's'
1	$l = 0$; 1s subshell	m = 0; s orbital no. of orbitals in s–subshell = 1	+ ½ & –½ no. of e's in s–subshell = 2
	Total no. of subshells in I shell = 1	**Total no. of orbitals in I shell = 1**	**Total no. of e's in I shell = 2**
2	$l = 0$; 2s subshell	m = 0; s orbital no. of orbitals in s–subshell = 1	+ ½ & – ½ no. of e's in s–subshell = 2
	$l = 1$; 2p subshell	m = –1; p_x / p_z m = 0; p_y m = +1; p_z / p_x no. of orbitals in p–subshell = 3	+ ½ & – ½ + ½ & – ½ + ½ & – ½ no. of e's in p–subshell = 6
	Total no. of subshells in II shell= 2	**Total no. of orbitals in II shell = 4**	**Total no. of e's in II shell = 8**
3	$l = 0$; 3s subshell	m = 0; s orbital no. of orbitals in s–subshell = 1	+ ½ & – ½ no. of e's in s–subshell = 2
	$l = 1$; 3p subshell	m = –1; p_x / p_z m = 0; p_y m = +1; p_z / p_x no. of orbitals in p–subshell = 3	+ ½ & – ½ + ½ & – ½ + ½ & – ½ no. of e's in p–subshell = 6
	$l = 2$; 3d subshell	m = –2 m = –1 m = 0 m = +1 m = +2 no. of orbital in d–subshell = 5	+ ½ & – ½ + ½ & – ½ + ½ & – ½ + ½ & – ½ + ½ & – ½ no. of e's in d–subshell = 10
	Total no. of subshells in III shell=3	**Total no. of orbitals in III shell = 9**	**Total no. of e's in III shell = 18**
4	$l = 0$; 4s subshell	m = 0; s orbital no. of orbitals in s–subshell = 1	+ ½ & – ½ no. of e's in s–subshell = 2
	$l = 1$; 4p subshell	m = –1; p_x / p_z m = 0; p_y m = +1; p_z / p_x no. of orbital in p–subshell = 3	+ ½ & – ½ + ½ & – ½ + ½ & – ½ no. of e's in p–subshell = 6
	$l = 2$; 4d subshell	m = –2 m = –1 m = 0 m = +1 m = +2 no. of orbitals in d–subshell = 5	+ ½ & – ½ + ½ & –½ + ½ & – ½ + ½ & – ½ + ½ & – ½ no. of e's in d–subshell = 10
	$l = 3$; 4f subshell	m = –3 m = –2 m = –1 m = 0 m = +1 m = +2 m = +3 no. of orbitals in f–subshell = 7	+ ½ & – ½ + ½ & – ½ + ½ & – ½ + ½ & – ½ + ½ & – ½ + ½ & – ½ + ½ & – ½ no. of e's in f–subshell = 14
	Total no. of subshells in IV shell = 4	**Total no. of orbitals in IV shell = 1+3+5+7=16**	**Total no. of e's in IV shell = 2+6+10+14=32**

From the above table we have derived the formula, to know the number of subshells/orbitals/electrons in a shell/subshell.

1. Total number of subshells in a particular shell = 'n'
2. Total number of orbitals in a particular subshell = $(2l + 1)$
3. Total number of orbitals in a particular shell = n^2
4. Total number of electrons in a particular subshell = $2(2l + 1)$
5. Total number of electrons in a particular shell = $2n^2$

3.1 NODE AND NODAL PLANE

Node is defined as a region where the probability of finding an electron is zero. Nodes can be of two types.

(a) Radial node or spherical node

(b) Angular node or planar node

Radial node or spherical node

They correspond to 'n' values i.e. as the distance between nucleus & outermost shell increase, the number of radial nodes increases. For example 1s, 2p, 3d & 4f orbital are closest to nucleus ($\because$ 1p, 1d, 2d, 1f, 2f, 3f doesnot exist) so there is no radial node but for higher values of 'n', radial nodes can be defined.

Angular node or planar node

They correspond to 'l' value. It depends upon the shape of orbitals. For example,

's' orbitals are spherically symmetrical in all three planes; so in s−orbital, no angular node exists. p−orbitals are not spherically symmetrical but the electron density is concentrated in one plane either x, y or z. So they have one angular node. Similarly electron density in d−orbital is concentrated in two planes i.e. xy, yz, zx etc. So the d−orbitals have two angular nodes.

Total no. of radial nodes = $(n - l - 1)$

Total no. of angular nodes = l

Total no. of nodes = $(n - l - 1) + l = n - 1$

3.2 SHAPES OF ATOMIC ORBITALS

(i) **s−orbital:** An electron is considered to be smeared out in the form of a cloud. The shape of the cloud is the shape of the orbital. The cloud is not uniform but denser in the region where the probability of finding the electron in maximum.

The orbital with the lowest energy is the 1s orbital. It is a sphere with its center at the nucleus of the atom. The s−orbital is said to spherically symmetrical about the nucleus, so that the electronic charge is not concentrated in any particular direction.

2s orbital is also spherically symmetrical about the nucleus, but it is larger than (i.e., away from) the 1s orbital.

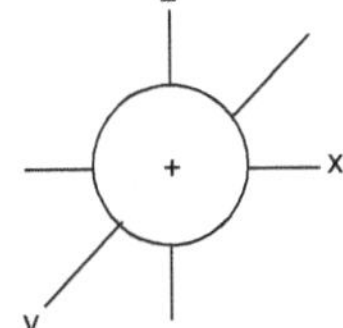

Shape of s−orbital

(ii) **p−orbitals:** There are three p−orbitals: p_x, p_y and p_z. They are dumb−bell shaped, the two levels being separated by a nodal plane, i.e., a plane where there is no likely hood of finding the electron. The p−orbitals have a marked directional character, depending on whether p_x, p_y and p_z orbital is being considered. The p−orbitals consist of two lobes with the atomic nucleus lying between them. The axis of each p−orbital is perpendicular to the other two. The p_x, p_y and p_z orbitals are equivalent except for their directional property. They have the same energy. Orbitals having the same energy are said to be degenerate.

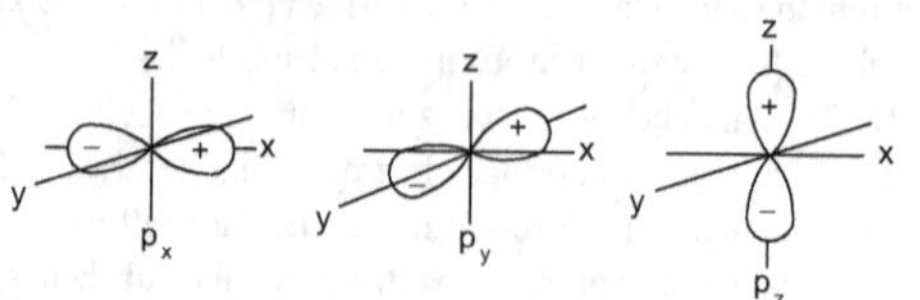

Shapes of p–orbital

(iii) **d–orbitals:** There are five d–orbitals. The shapes of four d–orbitals resemble four leaf cloves. The fifth d–orbital loops differently. The shapes of these orbitals are given below.

Illustration 5

Question: **Show that the circumference of an orbit of Bohr hydrogen atom is an integral multiple of the de Broglie wavelength associates with the electron revolving round the nucleus.**

Solution: According to Bohr's postulates,

$$mvr = \frac{nh}{2\pi}$$

$\therefore$ the circumference, $2\pi r = \dfrac{nh}{mv}$

From de Broglie's equation, $\lambda = \dfrac{h}{mv}$

$\therefore$ **$2\pi r = n\lambda$**

Illustration 6

Question: **(a) If a 1 g body is traveling along the x–axis with an uncertainity in velocity of 1 cm/s, what is minimum theoretical uncertainity in its position? (b) If an electron is traveling with uncertainity in velocity of 1 m/s, what is the minimum theoretical uncertainity in its position?**

Solution: (a) According to the uncertainity principle

$$\Delta x \times m\, \Delta v \geq \frac{h}{4\pi}$$

$$\Delta x \geq \frac{h}{4\pi m \Delta v}$$

$$\geq \frac{6.626 \times 10^{-27} \text{ ergs sec}}{4 \times 3.14 \times 1\,g \times 1\,cms^{-1}}$$

$$\geq 5.275 \times 10^{-28} \text{ cm} = 5.275 \times 10^{-30} \text{ m}$$

(b) $$\Delta x \geq \frac{6.626 \times 10^{-34} \text{ Js}}{4 \times 3.14 \times 9.1 \times 10^{-31}\,kg \times 1\,ms^{1}}$$

$$\geq 5.797 \times 10^{-5} \text{ m}.$$

PROFICIENCY TEST– II

The following 10 questions deal with the basic concepts of this section. Answer the following briefly. Go to the next section only if your score is greater than or equal to 8.
Do not consult the study material while attempting the questions.

1. Intensity of light is proportional to the_________ of electrons emitted.

2. Frequency of light is proportional to the _________ of electrons emitted.

3. (True/False): Stopping potential is measure of the maximum kinetic energy of the electrons.

4. The minimum frequency of light that is required for ejecting electron from an atom is called _________ .

5. (True/False): A single photon excites only a single electron.

6. (True/False): An electron can absorb more than one photon, simultaneously.

7. According to de Broglie the wavelength of a particle is given by $\lambda =$ _________ .

8. The minimum value of the product of uncertainity in position and momentum is _________ .

9. The shape of p–orbital is _________ .

10. (True/False) The energy of s–orbital is lower than the energy of p–orbital in same shell.

ANSWERS TO PROFICIENCY TEST– II

1. number

2. Energy

3. True

4. Threshold frequency

5. True

6. False

7. $\dfrac{h}{mv}$

8. $\dfrac{h}{4\pi}$

9. Dumb–bell

10. True

SOLVED OBJECTIVE EXAMPLES

Example 1:

Bohr's atomic model can explain
- (a) the spectrum of hydrogen atom only
- (b) the spectrum of an atom or ion containing one electron only
- (c) the spectrum of hydrogen molecule
- (d) the solar spectrum.

Solution:

In Bohr's theory while calculating the energy of electron, the potential energy has been found out by considering only the attraction between the electron and nucleus. If there is another electron in the orbit, the potential energy would change due electron–electron repulsion. Therefore the Bohr's model is meant for all one–electron systems.

$\therefore$ (b)

Example 2:

The orbital angular momentum of an electron in 2s orbital is
- (a) 4
- (b) 1
- (c) Zero
- (d) $\dfrac{h}{2\pi}$

Solution:

The orbital angular momentum of an electron is calculated as $\sqrt{l(l+1)}\dfrac{h}{2\pi}$.

$$\sqrt{0(0+1)}\,\frac{h}{2\pi} = 0$$

$\therefore$ (c)

Example 3:

The ratio of the energies of photons of 2000 Å to that of 4000 Å is
- (a) 2
- (b) 4
- (c) $\dfrac{1}{2}$
- (d) $\dfrac{1}{4}$

Solution:

$$E = \frac{hc}{\lambda}, \;\; \therefore \;\; \frac{E_1}{E_2} = \frac{\lambda_2}{\lambda_1} = \frac{4000}{2000} = 2$$

$\therefore$ (a)

Example 4:

Which of the following postulates does not belong to Bohr's model of the atom?
- (a) Angular momentum is an integral multiple of $\dfrac{h}{2\pi}$
- (b) The electron stationed in the orbit is stable.
- (c) The path of an electron is circular.
- (d) The change in the energy levels of electron is continuous.

Solution:

In Bohr's model, the energy levels are discrete and not continuous.

$\therefore$ (d)

Example 5:

The wave number of the first Balmer line of Li^{2+} ion is 1, 36, 800 cm^{-1}. The wave number of the first line of Balmer series of hydrogen atom is (in cm^{-1})
- (a) 68,400
- (b) 15,200
- (c) 76,000
- (d) 30,800

Solution:

Atomic number of Li^{2+} is 3

$$\frac{1}{\lambda} = R_H Z^2 \left[\frac{1}{n_1^2} - \frac{1}{n_2^2} \right]$$

$$1,36,800 = R_H \times 9 \left[\frac{1}{2^2} - \frac{1}{3^2} \right]$$

$$R_H \left[\frac{1}{2^2} - \frac{1}{3^2} \right] = \frac{1,36,800}{9} = 15,200$$

$\therefore$ (b)

Example 6:

If uncertainity in the position of an electron is zero the uncertainity in its momentum will be

(a) $< \dfrac{h}{4\pi}$

(b) $> \dfrac{h}{4\pi}$

(c) Zero

(d) infinite

Solution:

$$\Delta x \times \Delta p \geq \frac{h}{4\pi}$$

if $\Delta x = 0$, then Δp will be infinite

$\therefore$ (d)

Example 7:

The principal quantum number represents
(a) shape of an orbital
(b) number of electrons in an orbital
(c) distance of an electron from the nucleus
(d) orientation of orbitals in space

Solution:

$\therefore$ (c)

Example 8:

The energy of an electron of $2p_y$ orbital is
(a) greater than $2p_x$ orbital
(b) less than $2p_z$ orbital
(c) equal to 2s orbital
(d) same as that of $2p_x$ and $2p_z$ orbitals

Solution:

All the 2p orbitals are degenerate.

$\therefore$ (d)

Example 9:

If the following matter waves travel with equal velocity, the longest wavelength is that of a/an
(a) electron
(b) proton
(c) neutron
(d) α–particle

Solution:

$$\lambda = \frac{h}{mv}$$

λ will be large if m is small.

$\therefore$ (a)

Example 10:

Number of nodal planes (planes of zero electron density) in the d_{xy} orbital is
(a) 1

(b) 2

(c) 0

(d) 4

Solution:

xz & yz are planes with zero electron density for d_{xy} orbital.

$\therefore$ (b)

SOLVED SUBJECTIVE EXAMPLES

Example 1:

An electron in a Bohr orbit of hydrogen atom in quantum level n_2 has an angular momentum of 4.276 $\times$ 6 $\times 10^{-34}$ kgm^2 sec^{-1}. If this electron drops from this level to the next lower level, find the wavelength of this spectral line. (given $R_H = 109679$ cm^{-1})

Solution:

According to Bohr's theory

$$mvr = \frac{nh}{2\pi}$$

$$mvr = 4.2176 \times 10^{-34} \text{ kg m}^2\text{s}^{-1}$$

$$n = \frac{2 \times 3.14 \times (4.2176 \times 10^{-34}\,\text{kg m}^2\text{s}^{-1})}{(6.626 \times 10^{-34}\,\text{Js})}$$

$$= 3.99$$

$$\approx 4$$

when an electron falls from $n = 4$ to $n = 3$ in a hydrogen atom, the wavelength emitted is calculated as,

$$\frac{1}{\lambda} = R_H\left[\frac{1}{n_1^2} - \frac{1}{n_2^2}\right]$$

$$= 109679\left[\frac{1}{3^2} - \frac{1}{4^2}\right]$$

$$\lambda = 1.8756 \times 10^{-4} \text{ cm}^{-1}$$

$$= 1.8756 \times 10^{-6} \text{ m}^{-1}$$

$$= 18756 \times 10^{-10} \text{ m}^{-1}$$

$$= 18756 \text{ Å}$$

Example 2:

What transition in the hydrogen spectrum would have the same wavelength as the Balmer transition, $n = 4$ to $n = 2$ of He$^+$ spectrum?

Solution:

In the He$^+$ spectrum,

$$\frac{1}{\lambda} = R_H Z^2\left[\frac{1}{2^2} - \frac{1}{4^2}\right] \quad (\because Z = 2)$$

$$\frac{1}{\lambda} = R_H \times 4 \times \left[\frac{1}{2^2} - \frac{1}{4^2}\right]$$

In the hydrogen spectrum

$$\frac{1}{\lambda} = R_H\left[\frac{1}{n_1^2} - \frac{1}{n_2^2}\right]$$

For same wavelength,

$$R_H\left[\dfrac{1}{n_1^2}-\dfrac{1}{n_2^2}\right]=R_H\times4\times\left[\dfrac{1}{2^2}-\dfrac{1}{4^2}\right]$$

$$=R_H\times\left[\dfrac{1}{1^2}-\dfrac{1}{2^2}\right]$$

$$\therefore\ n_2=2,\ n_1=1$$

Example 3:

The circumference of the first Bohr orbit in H atom is 3.322×10^{-10} m. What is the velocity of the electron in this orbit?

Solution:

According to Bohr's model,

$$mvr=\dfrac{nh}{2\pi}$$

$$v=\dfrac{nh}{2\pi mr}=\dfrac{1\times(6.626\times10^{-34}\,Js)}{(9.1\times10^{-31}kg)\times3.322\times10^{-10}m}$$

$$=2.19\times10^6\text{ m/s}$$

Example 4:

How much will be the kinetic energy and total energy change of an e^- in H atom if the atom emits a photon of wavelength 4860Å?

Solution:

The energy released is

$$E=\dfrac{hc}{\lambda}=\dfrac{(6.62\times10^{-34}\,Js)(3\times10^8\,ms^{-1})}{(4860\times10^{-10}m)}=4.09\times10^{-19}\text{ J}$$

$\therefore$ Total energy change $= \mathbf{4.09\times10^{-19}\ J}$

Total energy of electron in an atom $=$ –kinetic energy of electron in an atom.

Loss in energy due to release of photon $\qquad=$ gain in kinetic energy

$$=4.09\times10^{-19}\text{ J}$$

Example 5:

Calculate the energy emitted when electrons of 1.0 g atom of hydrogen undergo transition giving the spectral lines of lowest energy in the visible region of its atomic spectra.

$R_H=1.1\times10^7\text{ m}^{-1},\ c=3\times10^8\text{ m sec}^{-1}$ and $h=6.62\times10^{-34}\text{ J sec.}$

Solution:

For visible line spectrum, i.e., Balmer series $n_1=2$. Also for minimum energy transition $n_2=3$.

$$\because\qquad\dfrac{1}{\lambda}=R_H\left[\dfrac{1}{n_1^2}-\dfrac{1}{n_2^2}\right]\quad\text{for H–atom}$$

$$\therefore\qquad\dfrac{1}{\lambda}=R_H\left[\dfrac{1}{2^2}-\dfrac{1}{3^2}\right]$$

$$=1.1\times10^7\left[\dfrac{1}{4}-\dfrac{1}{9}\right]=1.1\times10^7\times\dfrac{5}{36}\text{ m}^{-1}$$

$$\therefore \quad \lambda = 6.55 \times 10^{-7} \text{ m}$$

$$E = \frac{hc}{\lambda} = \frac{6.62 \times 10^{-34} \times 3.0 \times 10^{8}}{6.55 \times 10^{-7}}$$

$$= 3.037 \times 10^{-19} \text{ Joule}$$

if N electrons show this transition in 1 g atom of H then

$$\text{Energy released} = E \times N$$

$$= 3.03 \times 10^{-19} \times 6.023 \times 10^{23}$$

$$= 18.29 \times 10^{4} \text{ J}$$

$$= \mathbf{182.9 \ kJ.}$$

Example 6:

The dissociation of O_2 into two normal atoms requires 498 kJ mol^{-1}. Oxygen also undergoes photochemical dissociation into one normal oxygen atom and one excited atom having 1.967 eV more energy than normal atom. What is the maximum wavelength effective for photochemical dissociation of O_2?

Solution:

$$O_2 \longrightarrow 2O$$

$$2O \longrightarrow O + O^{*} \ (O^{*} \text{ is excited oxygen atom})$$

For dissociation, total energy required per atom is

$$= \frac{498 \times 10^{3}}{6.023 \times 10^{23}} \text{ J per atom}$$

For exciting one atom energy required is $= 1.967 \times 1.6 \times 10^{-19}$ J

$$\text{Total energy require is} = \frac{498 \times 10^{3}}{6.023 \times 10^{23}} \text{ J} + 1.967 \times 1.6 \times 10^{-19} \text{ J}$$

$$E = \frac{hc}{\lambda}$$

$$\lambda = \frac{hc}{E}$$

$$\lambda = \frac{(6.626 \times 10^{-34} \text{ Js})(3 \times 10^{8} \text{ ms}^{-1})}{\dfrac{498 \times 10^{3}}{6.023 \times 10^{23}} \text{ J} + 1.967 \times 1.6 \times 10^{-19} \text{ J}}$$

$$= 1.7413 \times 10^{-7} \text{ m}$$

$$= \mathbf{1741.3 \ \text{\AA}}$$

Example 7:

Positronium consists of an electron and a positron (same mass, opposite charge) orbiting around their common center of mass. The spectrum is therefore expected to be hydrogen like, the difference arising from the mass differences. Calculate the wave number of the first three lines of Balmer series of positronium.

Solution:

The masses of the nucleus and the electron are comparable and in such systems the mass of the nucleus is also to be taken into account. In the energy equation, instead of the mass of the electron, the reduced mass is to be taken.

By definition, reduced mass μ is

$$\frac{1}{\mu} = \frac{1}{m} + \frac{1}{M}$$

m is the mass of the electron and M is the mass of the nucleus.

$$\mu = \frac{m \times M}{m + M}$$

Since the mass of positron = mass of electron,

$$\mu = \frac{m \times m}{2m} = \frac{m}{2}$$

Therefore with equation for Rydberg constant, for positronium is

$$R_{pos} = \frac{2\pi^2 \mu e^4 k^2}{h^3 c} = \frac{2\pi^2 (m/2) e^4 k^2}{h^3 c}$$

$$= \frac{R_H}{2}$$

$$= \frac{109737}{2} = 54868.5 \text{ cm}^{-1}$$

First line of Balmer series: $\bar{v}_1 = 54868.5 \left(\frac{1}{2^2} - \frac{1}{3^2} \right) = 7620.6 \text{ cm}^{-1}$

Second line: $\bar{v}_2 = 54868.5 \left(\frac{1}{2^2} - \frac{1}{4^2} \right) = 10288 \text{ cm}^{-1}$

Third line: $\bar{v}_3 = 54868.5 \left(\frac{1}{2^2} - \frac{1}{5^2} \right) = 11522 \text{ cm}^{-1}$

Example 8:

The circumference of the second Bohr orbit of electron in hydrogen atom 600 nm. Calculate the potential difference to which the electron has to be subjected so that the electron stops. The electron had the de Broglie wavelength corresponding to this circumference.

Solution:

$$mvr = \frac{nh}{2\pi}$$

$$2\pi r = \frac{nh}{mv} = n\lambda$$

$$\lambda = \frac{2\pi r}{n} = \frac{600}{2} = 300 \text{ nm}$$

$$\lambda = \frac{h}{mv}$$

$$v = \frac{h}{m\lambda}$$

If V_o is the voltage,

$$eV_o = \frac{1}{2}mv^2$$

$$= \frac{1}{2}m \times \frac{h^2}{m^2\lambda^2}$$

$$V_o = \frac{h^2}{2\,m\lambda^2 e}$$

$$= \frac{(6.626 \times 10^{-34}\,Js)^2}{2 \times (9.1 \times 10^{-31}\,kg) \times (300 \times 10^{-9}\,m)^2 \times (1.6 \times 10^{-19}\,C)}$$

$$= 1.675 \times 10^{-5}\,V$$

Example 9:

Calculate the retarding potential to be applied to an electron to increase its de Broglie wavelength of 1.75 Å to 2.25 Å?

Solution:

Wavelength change $= 2.25 - 1.75$

$$= 0.5\,Å$$

Energy decrease $= \dfrac{hc}{\lambda}$

$$= \frac{(6.626 \times 10^{-34}\,Js) \times (3 \times 10^8\,ms^{-1})}{(0.5 \times 10^{-10}\,m)}$$

$$= 3.975 \times 10^{-15}\,J$$

$$eV_o = E$$

$$(1.6 \times 10^{-19}\,C)\,V_o = 3.975 \times 10^{-15}$$

$$V_o = \frac{3.975 \times 10^{-15}}{1.6 \times 10^{-19}}$$

$$= 24843.75\,V$$

It looks very much logical to do it this way. But the mistake here is,

$$\lambda = \frac{c}{v}$$ is applicable only to electromagnetic waves and not to particle waves.

The correct method is:

$$\Delta E = \frac{1}{2}m(v_1^2 - v_2^2)$$

$$= \frac{1}{2}m\left[\left(\frac{h}{m\lambda_1}\right)^2 - \left(\frac{h}{m\lambda_2}\right)^2\right]$$

$$= \frac{1}{2}m\frac{h^2}{m^2}\left[\left(\frac{1}{\lambda_1}\right)^2 - \left(\frac{1}{\lambda_2}\right)^2\right]$$

$$= \frac{h^2}{2m}\left[1.29 \times 10^{19}\right]$$

$$eV_o = \Delta E$$

$$V_o = \frac{\Delta E}{e} = \frac{(6.626 \times 10^{-34}\,Js)^2 \times (1.29 \times 10^{19}\,m^{-2})}{2 \times (9.1 \times 10^{-31}\,kg)\,(1.6 \times 10^{-19}\,C)} = 19.45\,V$$

MIND MAP

1. According to the quantum theory, the radiant energy is emitted by atoms & molecules in small discrete amounts (quanta), rather than over a continuous range. The energy of each quanta is given by $E = h\nu$

2. According to Bohr model, the angular momentum of an electron is an integral multiple of $\dfrac{h}{2\pi}$. Bohr's model is applicable single electron species (hydrogen like species).

3. The radius of an orbit is given by $r = \dfrac{n^2 h^2}{4\pi^2 KZme^2}$. The velocity of an electron in an orbit is given by $v = \dfrac{nh}{2\pi mr}$ and the energy of an electron in an orbit is given by $E = \dfrac{-2\pi^2 K^2 Z^2 me^4}{n^2 h^2}$

9. In photoelectric effect, electrons are ejected from the surface of certain metal exposed to light of at least a certain minimum frequency called threshold frequency.
$h\nu = h\nu_\circ + K.E$

4. In Bohr model, an electron emits a photon when it drops from a higher energy state to a lower energy state.

ATOMIC STRUCTURE

8. Four quantum numbers characterize each electron in an atom. The principal quantum number(n) identifies the main energy level, the angular quantum number (l) indicates shape of orbital, the magnetic quantum number (m) specifies orientation of orbital in space and the spin quantum number (s) indicates the direction of the electron's spin on its axis.

5. The emission spectra of hydrogen is obtained when electron from an excited state is deexcited to the ground state. The release of specific amounts of energy in the form of photons accounts for the lines in the hydrogen spectrum. $\bar{\nu}$ of each line in the spectrum can be given by $\dfrac{1}{\lambda} = R_H z^2\left[\dfrac{1}{n_1^2} - \dfrac{1}{n_2^2}\right]$

7. An orbital may be defined as a region in space around the nucleus where the probability of finding the electron is maximum.

6. De Broglie extended Einstein's wave –particle description of light to all matters in motion. The wavelength of a moving particle of mass m and velocity ν is given by de Broglie equation, $\lambda = \dfrac{h}{m\nu}$.

EXERCISE – I

IIT JEE - SINGLE CHOICE CORRECT

1. A ball of mass 200 g moving with a velocity of 10 m sec^{-1}. If the error in measurement of velocity is 0.1%, the uncertainty in its position is
   (a) 3.3×10^{-31} m
   (b) 3.3×10^{-27} m
   (c) 5.3×10^{-25} m
   (d) 2.64×10^{-32} m

2. Which of the following set of quantum numbers represents an impossible arrangement?

	n	l	m	s
(a)	3	2	–2	–1/2
(b)	4	0	0	–1/2
(c)	3	2	–3	–1/2
(d)	5	3	0	–1/2

3. If the series limit of wavelength of the Lyman series for the hydrogen atoms in 912 Å, then the series limit of wavelength for the Balmer series of the hydrogen atom is
   (a) 912 Å
   (b) 912 × 2 Å
   (c) 912 × 4 Å
   (d) 912/2 Å

4. The shortest λ for the Lyman series of hydrogen atom is ….. (Given $R_H = 109678$ cm^{-1})
   (a) 911.7 Å
   (b) 700 Å
   (c) 600 Å
   (d) 811 Å

5. With increasing quantum number, the energy difference between adjacent orbits of hydrogen atom
   (a) increases
   (b) decreases
   (c) remains constant
   (d) first increases followed by a decrease

6. The number of orbitals in a subshell is equal to
   (a) n^2
   (b) $2l$
   (c) $2l + 1$
   (d) m

7. Ground state electronic configuration of nitrogen atom can be represented as

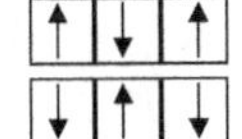

8. Which of the following set of quantum numbers belong to highest energy?
   (a) $n = 4, l = 0, m = 0, s = +\dfrac{1}{2}$
   (b) $n = 3, l = 0, m = 0, s = +\dfrac{1}{2}$
   (c) $n = 3, l = 1, m = 1, s = +\dfrac{1}{2}$
   (d) $n = 3, l = 2, m = 1, s = +\dfrac{1}{2}$

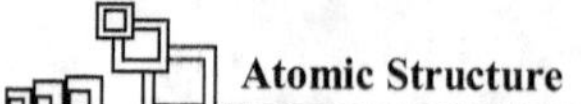

9. If the radius of first Bohr orbit is x, then de Broglie wavelength of electron in 3rd orbit is nearly
   (a) $2\pi x$
   (b) $6\pi x$
   (c) $9x$
   (d) $x/3$

10. In Bohr's hydrogen atom, the electronic transition emitting light of longest wavelength is
    (a) n = 4 to n = 5
    (b) n = 4 to n = 3
    (c) n = 3 to n = 2
    (d) n = 2 to n = 4

11. The frequency of first line of Balmer series in hydrogen atom is v_0. The frequency of corresponding line emitted by singly ionised helium atom is
    (a) $2v_0$
    (b) $4v_0$
    (c) $v_0/2$
    (d) $v_0/4$

12. The magnetic quantum number for valence electron of sodium is
    (a) 3
    (b) 2
    (c) 1
    (d) zero

13. The potential energy of the electron in an orbit of hydrogen atom would be
    (a) $-mv^2$
    (b) $-e^2/r^2$
    (c) $-1/2\ mv^2$
    (d) $-e^2/2r$

14. Which of the following radiations has the highest wave number?
    (a) X–rays
    (b) Microwaves
    (c) I. R. rays
    (d) Radiowaves

15. Which of the following particles moving with same velocity would be associated with smallest de–Broglie wavelength?
    (a) Hydrogen molecule
    (b) Oxygen molecule
    (c) Helium molecule
    (d) Nitrogen molecule

16. If the velocity of an electron in the first Bohr orbit of a hydrogen atom is V, then its velocity in the third Bohr orbit will be
    (a) V/9
    (b) V/3
    (c) 9 V
    (d) 3 V

17. What is the wavelength associated with an electron moving with a velocity of 10^6 m/s? (Given h = 6.63×10^{-34} Js and m = 9.11×10^{-28} g)
    (a) 72.8 nm
    (b) 0.728 nm
    (c) 7.28 nm
    (d) 7.28×10^{-13} m

18. If the ionization potential for hydrogen atom is 13.6 eV then the second ionization potential for helium atom should be
    (a) 13.6 eV
    (b) 27.2 eV
    (c) 54.4 eV
    (d) none of these

19. The ratio of the radius of Bohr first orbit for the electron orbiting the hydrogen nucleus to that of the electron orbiting the deuterium nucleus (mass nearly twice that of H nucleus) is approximately
    (a) 1 : 1
    (b) 1 : 2
    (c) 2 : 1
    (d) 1 : 4

20. Velocity of electron in the first orbit of H–atom as compared to that of velocity of light is nearly

(a) $\dfrac{1}{10}$ th

(b) $\dfrac{1}{100}$ th

(c) $\dfrac{1}{1000}$ th

(d) $\dfrac{1}{150}$ th

21. Assuming the velocity to be same, which sub–atomic particle possesses smallest de Broglie wavelength

(a) An electron

(b) A proton

(c) An α–particle

(d) All have same wavelength

22. An electron in H–atom in its ground state absorbs 1.50 times as much as energy as the minimum required for its escape (13.6 eV) from the atom. Thus KE given to emitted electron is

(a) 13.6 eV

(b) 20.4 eV

(c) 34.0 eV

(d) 6.8 eV

23. The velocity of an electron in a Bohr's orbit is

(a) $\propto \dfrac{1}{n}$

(b) $\propto n$

(c) $\propto n^2$

(d) $\propto \dfrac{1}{n^2}$

24. Bohr's theory is not valid for the species

(a) H atom

(b) He^+ ion

(c) Li^+ ion

(d) Li^{2+} ion

25. If wavelength of an electron is equal to distance travelled by it in one second, then correct relation is

(a) $\lambda = \dfrac{h}{p}$

(b) $\lambda = \sqrt{\dfrac{h}{p}}$

(c) $\lambda = \dfrac{h}{m}$

(d) $\lambda = \sqrt{\dfrac{h}{m}}$

EXERCISE – II

IIT-JEE & NEET - SINGLE CHOICE CORRECT

1. An electron, a proton and an alpha particle have kinetic energies of 16E, 4E and E respectively. What is the correct order of their de–Broglie wavelengths?

(a) $\lambda e > \lambda p \simeq \lambda \alpha$

(b) $\lambda p \simeq \lambda \alpha > \lambda e$

(c) $\lambda e > \lambda p > \lambda \alpha$

(d) $\lambda_\alpha < \lambda e > \lambda p$

2. Which of the following electronic transitions requires that the greatest quantity of energy be absorbed by a hydrogen atom?

(a) $n = 1$ to $n = 2$

(b) $n = 2$ to $n = 4$

(c) $n = 3$ to $n = 6$

(d) $n = \infty$ to $n = 1$

3. Which of the following statement regarding an orbital is correct?

(a) An orbital is a definite trajectory around the nucleus in which electron can move.

(b) An orbital always has spherical trajectory.

(c) It is the region around the nucleus where there is 90 to 95% probability of finding all the electrons in an atom.

(d) An orbital is characterized by three distinct quantum numbers n, l and m.

4. If uncertainty in position of an electron were zero, the uncertainty in its momentum would be

(a) Zero

(b) $h/2\pi$

(c) $h/4\pi$

(d) Infinity

5. When the frequency of light incident on a metallic plate is doubled above threshold frequency, the KE of the emitted photoelectrons will be

(a) doubled

(b) halved

(c) increased but will be more than double of the previous KE

(d) unchanged

6. The radius of H–atom in ground state is 0.53 Å. Radius of the first orbit of Li^{2+} in Å is

(a) 0.106

(b) 0.3

(c) 0.17

(d) 0.53

7. The amount of energy required to remove an electron from a Li^{2+} ion in its ground state is how many times the amount of energy required to remove the electron from a hydrogen atom in its ground state

(a) 9

(b) 2

(c) 3

(d) 5

8. In an atom, two electrons move around the nucleus in circular orbits of radii R and 4R. The ratio of the time taken by them to complete one revolution is

(a) 1 : 4

(b) 4 : 1

(c) 1 : 8

(d) 8 : 7

9. A $3p$–orbital has

(a) two angular nodes

(b) two radial nodes

(c) one radial and one angular node

(d) one radial and two angular nodes

10. Which of the following statement is not correct?
(a) The shape of an atomic orbital depends on the azimuthal quantum number.
(b) The orientation of an atomic orbital depends on the magnetic quantum number.
(c) The energy of an electron in an atomic orbital of multielectron atom depends on principal quantum number.
(d) The number of degenerate atomic orbitals of one type depends on the value of azimuthal quantum number.

11. The orbital angular momentum of an electron in 2s orbital is
(a) $h/4\pi$
(b) zero
(c) $h/2\pi$
(d) $\sqrt{2}\,\dfrac{h}{2\pi}$

12. The first emission line of Balmer series in H spectrum has the wave number equal to
(a) $\dfrac{9R_H}{400}$
(b) $\dfrac{7R_H}{144}$
(c) $\dfrac{3R_H}{4}$
(d) $\dfrac{5R_H}{36}$

13. The potential energy of the electron present in the ground state of Li^{2+} ion is represented by
(a) $+\dfrac{3e^2}{4\pi\varepsilon_0 r}$
(b) $-\dfrac{3e}{4\pi\varepsilon_0 r}$
(c) $-\dfrac{3e^2}{4\pi\varepsilon_0 r^2}$
(d) $-\dfrac{3e^2}{4\pi\varepsilon_0 r}$

14. If n and l are the principal and Azimuthal quantum numbers respectively, then the expression for calculating the maximum number of electrons in any orbit is
(a) $\displaystyle\sum_{l=1}^{l=n} 2(2l+1)$
(b) $\displaystyle\sum_{l=1}^{l=n-1} 2(2l+1)$
(c) $\displaystyle\sum_{l=0}^{l=n+1} 2(2l+1)$
(d) $\displaystyle\sum_{l=0}^{l=n-1} 2(2l+1)$

15. If λ_0 is the threshold wavelength of a metal and λ is the wavelength of the incident radiation, the maximum velocity of the ejected electrons from the metal would be
(a) $\left[\dfrac{2hc}{m}\left(\dfrac{\lambda_0-\lambda}{\lambda\lambda_0}\right)\right]^{1/2}$
(b) $\left[\dfrac{2hc}{m}\left(\dfrac{\lambda-\lambda_0}{\lambda\lambda_0}\right)\right]^{1/2}$
(c) $\left[2\dfrac{hc}{m}(\lambda_0-\lambda)\right]^{1/2}$
(d) $\left[\dfrac{2h}{m}(\lambda-\lambda_0)\right]^{1/2}$

16. If kinetic energy of a proton is increased to nine times, the wavelength of the de–Broglie wave associated with it would become
(a) 3 times
(b) 9 times
(c) $\dfrac{1}{3}$ times
(d) $\dfrac{1}{9}$ times

17. If r_1 is the radius of the first orbit of hydrogen atom, then the radii of second, third and fourth orbits in terms of r_1 are
(a) r_1^2, r_1^3, r_1^4
(b) $8r_1, 27r_1, 64r_1$
(c) $4r_1, 9r_1, 16r_1$
(d) $2r_1, 6r_1, 8r_1$

18. The difference in angular momentum associated with the electron in two successive orbits of hydrogen atom is

(a) h/π (b) $h/2\pi$

(c) $h/2$ (d) $(n-1)\,h/2\pi$

19. Difference between nth and (n + 1)th Bohr's radius of 'H' atom is equal to it's (n−1)th Bohr's radius. The value of n is

(a) 1

(b) 2

(c) 3

(d) 4

20. Total number of transitions of an electron from nth shell to 2nd shell will be

(a) $\dfrac{(n-1)(n-2)}{2}$

(b) $\dfrac{n(n-1)}{2}$

(c) $\dfrac{n(n+1)}{2}$

(d) $\dfrac{n}{2}$

ONE OR MORE THAN ONE CHOICE CORRECT

1. The radius of the following orbits are double as that of the first Bohr's orbit of hydrogen atom.

(a) He^+ (n = 2)

(b) Be^{+3} (n = 2)

(c) O^{+7} (n = 4)

(d) C^{+5} (n = 3)

2. Which of the following statements are incorrect in relation to energies of orbitals?

(a) Energy of an electron in a hydrogen atom is determined solely by the principal quantum number.

(b) Energy of an electron in a multi electron atoms, depends on both, principal and azimuthal quantum number.

(c) Energy of the orbitals in the same subshell increase with increase in the atomic number.

(d) Higher the value of $(n + l)$ for an orbital lower is its energy.

3. Which of the following are correct statements?

(a) Hund's rule deals with degenerate orbitals.

(b) Pauli's exclusion principle stated that only two electrons may exist in one orbital and these electrons must have opposite spin.

(c) In ground state of atom, the orbitals are filled on the basis of increasing $(n + l)$ value.

(d) The maximum number of electrons in the subshell with principal quantum number 'n' is equal to $2n^2$?

4. If uncertainty in momentum is twice the uncertainty in position of an electron, then uncertainty in velocity is, $\left(\hbar = \dfrac{h}{2\pi}\right)$

(a) $\dfrac{h}{4\pi m}$

(b) $\sqrt{\dfrac{h}{2\pi m^2}}$

(c) $\dfrac{1}{m}\sqrt{\hbar}$

(d) $\dfrac{1}{2m}\sqrt{\hbar}$

5. Which of the following statements are correct?

(a) Electronic configuration of Cu is [Ar] $3d^9 4s^1$. (atomic number of Cu = 29)

(b) Magnetic quantum number may have negative value.

(c) In copper atom, 14 electrons have spin one type and 15 of the opposite type.

(d) Spin multiplicity of copper is two.

6. Which of the following statements are not correct about atomic orbital?

(a) Size of the atomic orbital depends on the azimuthal quantum number.

(b) Shape of the atomic orbital depends on both principal and azimuthal quantum number.

(c) Orientation of an atomic orbital depends on the spin quantum number.

(d) Rotation of an electron in an atomic orbital depends on Heisenberg uncertainty principal.

7. Which of the following sets of quantum numbers are correct for a 3d electron?

(a) $3, 2, 1, -\dfrac{1}{2}$ (b) $3, -2, -1, +\dfrac{1}{2}$

(c) $3, 2, -2, +\dfrac{1}{2}$ (d) $3, 2, 0, -\dfrac{1}{2}$

8. Which of the following statements do not form a part of Bohr's model of hydrogen atom?

(a) Splitting of spectral lines takes place in electric and magnetic field.

(b) Energy of the electron in the orbit is not quantized.

(c) Angular momentum of the electron in the orbit is quantized.

(d) The radius and velocity of the electron in the orbit can be determined simultaneously.

9. The wavelength of the spectral line for an electronic transition depends on

(a) the nuclear charge of the ion containing only one electron.

(b) velocity of electron in an atom undergoing transition.

(c) difference in the energy levels involved in the transition.

(d) circumference of the orbits in which transition taking place.

10. Choose the correct statements from among the following

(a) The total number of spherical nodes in an orbital are $n - l - 1$.

(b) The total number of angular nodes in an orbital are l.

(c) The number of maxima in the plot between ψ^2 vs r for an orbital is $(n - l)$.

(d) A node is a point in space where the wave function ψ has zero amplitude.

EXERCISE – V

MATCH THE FOLLOWING

1.

Column I (For mono electronic species)	Column II
I. Radius of nth orbit	**(A)** inversely proportional to Z
II. Energy of electron in nth orbit	**(B)** inversely proportional to n^2
III. Velocity of electron in nth orbit	**(C)** inversely proportional to n
IV. Angular momentum of electron	**(D)** proportional to n
	(E) proportional to n^2

REASONING TYPE

Directions: Read the following questions and choose

    (A) If both the statements are true and statement-2 is the correct explanation of **statement-1**.

    (B) If both the statements are true but statement-2 is not the correct explanation of **statement-1**.

    (C) If statement-1 is True and **statement-2** is False.

    (D) If statement-1 is False **and statement-2** is True.

1.   **Statement-1**:   Bohr's orbits are called stationary orbits.

       Statement-2:   Electrons donot move in these orbits.

       (a) (A)   (b) (B)   (c) (C)   (d) (D)

2.   **Statement-1**:   If an electron is located within the range of 0.1 Å then the uncertainly in velocity is approximately 6×10^6 m/sec.

       Statement-2:   Trajectory of above can be defined.

       (a) (A)   (b) (B)   (c) (C)   (d) (D)

3.   **Statement-1**:   Hydrogen has only one electron in its orbit but produces several spectral lines.

       Statement-2:   There are many excited energy levels available.

       (a) (A)   (b) (B)   (c) (C)   (d) (D)

4.   **Statement-1**:   An orbital cannot have more than two electrons.

       Statement-2:   The two electrons in an orbital create opposite magnetic field.

       (a) (A)   (b) (B)   (c) (C)   (d) (D)

5.   **Statement-1**:   The radial probability of 1s electron first increases, till it is maximum at 0.529 Å and then decreases.

       Statement-2:   Bohr's radius for the first orbit is 0.529 Å.

       (a) (A)   (b) (B)   (c) (C)   (d) (D)

LINKED COMPREHENSION TYPE

The only electron in the hydrogen atom residue under ordinary conditions on the first orbit. When energy is supplied, the electron moves to higher energy orbit depending on the amount of energy absorbed. When this electron returns to any of the lower orbits, it emits energy. Lyman series is formed when the electron returns to the lowest orbit while Balmer series is formed when the electron returns to second orbit. Similarly, Paschen, Brackett and Pfund series are formed when electron returns to the third, fourth and fifth orbits from higher energy orbits respectively.

Maximum number of lines produced when an electron jumps from nth level to ground level is equal to $\dfrac{n(n-1)}{2}$. For example, in the case of n = 4, number of lines produced is 6. $(4 \rightarrow 3, 4 \rightarrow 2, 4 \rightarrow 1, 3 \rightarrow 2, 3 \rightarrow 1, 2 \rightarrow 1)$. When an electron returns from n_2 to n_1 state, the number of lines in the spectrum will be equal to

$$\dfrac{(n_2 - n_1)(n_2 - n_1 + 1)}{2}$$

If the electron comes back from energy level having energy E_2 to energy level having energy E_1, then the difference may be expressed in terms of energy of photon as:

$$E_2 - E_1 = \Delta E, \quad \lambda = \dfrac{hc}{\Delta E}$$

Since h and c are constants, ΔE corresponds to definite energy; thus each transition from one energy level to another will produce a light of definite wavelength. This is actually observed as a line in the spectrum of hydrogen atom.

Wave number of line is given by the formula $\bar{v} = RZ^2 \left(\dfrac{1}{n_1^2} - \dfrac{1}{n_2^2} \right)$.

Where R is a Rydberg constant

1. In a single isolated atom an electron makes transition from 5th excited state to 2nd state then maximum number of different types of photons observed is
   (a) 3
   (b) 4
   (c) 6
   (d) 15

2. The difference in the wavelength of the 2nd line of Lyman series and last line of bracket series in a hydrogen sample is
   (a) $\dfrac{119}{8R}$
   (b) $\dfrac{1271}{8R}$
   (c) $\dfrac{219}{8R}$
   (d) None of these

3. The wave number of electromagnetic radiation emitted during the transition of electron in between two levels of Li^{2+} ion whose principal quantum numbers sum is 4 and difference is 2 is
   (a) $3.5\,R_H$
   (b) $4\,R_H$
   (c) $8\,R_H$
   (d) $\dfrac{8}{9}\,R_H$

EXERCISE – IV

SUBJECTIVE PROBLEMS

1. The Schrodinger wave equation for hydrogen atom is

$$\psi_{2s} = \frac{1}{4\sqrt{2\pi}} \left(\frac{1}{a_o} \right)^{3/2} \left[2 - \frac{r_o}{a_o} \right] e^{-r/a_o}$$

   where a_o is Bohr radius. If the radial node in 2s be at r_o, then find r_o in terms of a_o.

2. Consider the hydrogen atom to be a proton embedded in a cavity of radius a_0 (Bohr radius) whose charge is neutralized by the addition of an electron to the cavity in vacuum infinitely slowly. Estimate the average total energy of an electron in its ground state in a hydrogen atom as the work done in the above neutralization process. Also, if the magnitude of average KE is half the magnitude of average potential energy, find the average potential energy.

3. When a certain metal was irradiated with light of frequency 3.2×10^{16} Hz, the photoelectrons emitted has twice the kinetic energy as did photoelectrons emitted when the same metal was irradiated with light of frequency 2.0×10^{16} Hz. Calculate v_0 for the metal.

4. Calculate the energy required to excite 1.23 litre of hydrogen gas at 1 atm and 300 K to the first excited state of atomic hydrogen. The energy for the dissociation of H–H bond is 436 kJ mol^{-1}. Also calculate the minimum frequency of photon to break this bond.

5. A certain dye absorbs light of $\lambda = 4530$ Å and then fluorescence light of wavelength 5080 Å. Assuming that under given conditions 47% of the absorbed energy is re–emitted out as fluorescence, calculate the ratio of quanta emitted out to the number of quanta absorbed.

6. The ionisation potential of H is 13.6 eV. It is exposed to electromagnetic waves of 1028 Å and gives out induced radiations. Find the wavelength of these induced radiations.

7. Wavelength of high energy transition of H atom is 91.2 nm. Calculate the corresponding wavelength of He^+ ion.

8. Find out the number of waves made by a Bohr electron in one complete revolution in its 3rd orbit.

9. The photo electric emission requires a threshold frequency v_0. For a certain metal $\lambda_1 = 2200$ Å and $\lambda_2 = 1900$ Å produce electrons with a maximum kinetic energy KE_1 and KE_2, if $KE_2 = 2KE_1$. Calculate v_0.

10. Find out the following:
    (a) The velocity of electron in first Bohr orbit of H–atom ($r = a_0$).
    (b) de Broglie wavelength of the electron in first Bohr orbit of H–atom.
    (c) The orbital angular momentum of 2p–orbitals in terms of $\dfrac{h}{2\pi}$ units.

ANSWERS

EXERCISE – I

IIT JEE - SINGLE CHOICE CORRECT

1. (d)	2. (c)	3. (c)	4. (a)	5. (b)
6. (c)	7. (a)	8. (d)	9. (b)	10. (b)
11. (b)	12. (d)	13. (a)	14. (a)	15. (b)
16. (b)	17. (b)	18. (c)	19. (a)	20. (d)
21. (c)	22. (d)	23. (a)	24. (c)	25. (d)

EXERCISE – II

IIT-JEE & NEET-SINGLE CHOICE CORRECT

1. (a)	2. (a)	3. (d)	4. (d)	5. (c)
6. (c)	7. (a)	8. (c)	9. (c)	10. (c)
11. (b)	12. (d)	13. (d)	14. (d)	15. (a)
16. (c)	17. (c)	18. (b)	19. (d)	20. (a)

ONE OR MORE THAN ONE CHOICE CORRECT

1. (a, c)	2. (c, d)	3. (a, b, c)	4. (b, c)	5. (b, c, d)
6. (a,b,c,d)	7. (a,c,d)	8. (a, b)	9. (a, c)	10. (a,b,c,d)

EXERCISE – III

MATCH THE FOLLOWING

1. I – (A), (E) ; II – (B) ; III – (C) ; IV – (D)

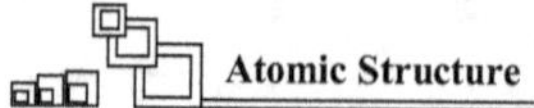

REASONING TYPE

1. (c)	2. (c)	3. (a)	4. (b)	5. (b)

LINKED COMPREHENSION TYPE

1. (a)	2. (a)	3. (c)

EXERCISE – IV

SUBJECTIVE PROBLEMS

1. $2a_0$.

2. $-\dfrac{1}{4\pi\varepsilon_0}\dfrac{Ze^2}{a_0}$

3. 8.0×10^{15} Hz.

4. 120 kJ ; 1.09×10^{15} sec^{-1} or Hz

5. 0.527

6. $\lambda = 1028\,\text{Å}$; $\lambda = 1216\,\text{Å}$; $\lambda = 6568\,\text{Å}$

7. 22.8 nm

8. 3

9. 1.148×10^{15} sec^{-1}

10. (a) 2.19×10^8 cm/sec (b) $3.32\,\text{Å}$ (c) $\sqrt{2}\times\hbar\left(\hbar=\dfrac{h}{2\pi}\right)$

Single Correct Answer Type

1. The lightest particle is
   1) -particle
   2) Positron
   3) Proton
   4) Neutron

2. The number of electrons and protons in an atoms of third alkaline earth metal is
   1) $e\ 20, p\ 20$
   2) $e\ 18, p\ 20$
   3) $e\ 18, p\ 18$
   4) $e\ 19, p\ 20$

3. Increasing order (lowest first) for the values of e/m for electron (e), proton (p), neutron (n) and α-particles is
   1) e, p, n, α
   2) n, α, p, e
   3) n, p, e, α
   4) n, p, α, e

4. Nuclear theory of the atom was put forward by
   1) Rutherford
   2) Aston
   3) Neils Bohr
   4) J.J. Thomson

5. A heavy element has atomic number X and mass number Y. Correct relationship between X and Y is
   1) XY
   2) XY
   3) XY
   4) $XZ(1\ Y)^2$

6. Which one of the following groupings represents a collection of isoelectronic species? (At. no. Cs=55, Br=35)
   1) Na, Ca^2, Mg^2
   2) N^3, F, Na
   3) Be, Al^3, Cl
   4) Ca^2, Cs, Br

7. Particle nature of electron was experimentally demonstrated by
   1) Max Bon
   2) J.J. Thomson
   3) De-Broglie
   4) Schrondinger

8. Common name for proton and neutron is
   1) Deutron
   2) Positron
   3) Meson
   4) Nucleon

9. The compound in which cation is isoelectronic with anion is
   1) $NaCl$
   2) CsF
   3) NaI
   4) K_2S

10. Which has the highest e/m ratio?
    1) He^{2+}
    2) H^+
    3) He^+
    4) D^+

11. Isotopes are
    1) Atoms of different elements having same mass number
    2) Atoms of same elements having same mass number
    3) Atoms of same elements having different mass number
    4) Atoms of different elements having same number of neutrons

12. Number of neutron in C^{12} is
    1) 6
    2) 7
    3) 8
    4) 9

13. The nucleus of an atom contains
    1) Proton and electron
    2) Neutron and electron
    3) Proton and neutron
    4) Proton, neutron and electron

14. Which particle contains 2 neutrons and 1 proton?
    1) $_1H^2$
    2) $_2He^4$
    3) $_1T^3$
    4) $_1D^2$

15. The charge on an electron was discovered by
    1) J.J. Thomson
    2) Neil Bohr
    3) James Chadwick
    4) Mullikan

16. Which one of the following ions is not isoelectronic with O^{2-}?
    1) Ti^+
    2) Na^+
    3) F^-
    4) N^{3-}

17. Mg^{2+} is isoelectrionic with
    1) Cu^{2+}
    2) Zn^{2+}
    3) Na^+
    4) Ca^{2+}

18. What is the ration of mass of an electron to the mass of a proton?
    1) 1:2
    2) 1:1
    3) 1:1837
    4) 1:3

19. An isobar of $_{20}Ca^{40}$ is
    1) $_{18}Ar^{40}$
    2) $_{20}Ca^{38}$
    3) $_{20}Ca^{42}$
    4) $_{18}Ar^{38}$

20. The electronic configuration of a dipositive ion M^{2+} is 2, 8, 14 and its mass number is 56. The number of neutrons present is
    1) 32
    2) 42
    3) 30
    4) 34

21. Which of the following make up an isotonic triad?
    1) $_{32}^{78}Ge, _{33}^{77}As, _{31}^{74}Ga$
    2) $_{18}^{40}Ar, _{19}^{40}K, _{20}^{40}Ca$
    3) $_{92}^{233}U, _{90}^{232}Th, _{94}^{239}Pu$
    4) $_{6}^{13}C, _{7}^{12}C, _{7}^{14}N$
    5) $_{6}^{14}C, _{8}^{16}O, _{7}^{15}N$

22. Isoelectronic pair among the following is
    1) Ca and K
    2) Ar and Ca^{2+}
    3) K and Ca^{2+}
    4) Ar and K

23. Which one of the following has unit positive charge and 1 u mass?
    1) Electron
    2) Neutron
    3) Proton
    4) None of these

24. The triad of nuclei which is isotonic is
    1) $_{6}^{14}C, _{7}^{14}N, _{9}^{17}F$
    2) $_{6}^{14}C, _{7}^{14}N, _{9}^{19}F$
    3) $_{6}^{14}C, _{7}^{15}N, _{9}^{17}F$
    4) $_{6}^{12}C, _{7}^{14}N, _{9}^{19}F$

25. Which one of the following sets of ions represents a collection of isoelectronic species?
    1) $K^+, Cl^-, Ca^{2+}, Sc^{3+}$
    2) $Ba^{2+}, Sr^{2+}, K^+, S^{2-}$
    3) $N^{3-}, O^{2-}, F^-, S^{2-}$
    4) $Li^+, Na^+, Mg^{2+}, Ca^{2+}$

26. Ca^2 is isoelectronic with
    1) Na
    2) Ar
    3) Mg^2
    4) Kr

27. The electronic configuration of an element in ultimate and penultimate orbitals is $(n-1)s^2(n-1)p^6(n-1)d^x ns^2$. If $n=4$ and $x=5$ then number of protons in the nucleus is
    1) 25
    2) <724
    3) 25
    4) 30

28. Which of the following is correct?
    1) $_1H^1$ and $_2He^3$ are isotopes
    2) $_6C^{14}$ and $_7N^{14}$ are isotopes
    3) $_{19}K^{39}$ and $_{20}Ca^{40}$ are isotones
    4) $_9F^{19}$ and $_{11}Na^{24}$ are isodiaphers

29. How many neutrons are present in tritium nucleus?
   1) 2
   2) 3
   3) 1
   4) 0

30. An isotone of $^{76}_{32}Ge$ is
   1) $^{77}_{32}Ge$
   2) $^{77}_{33}As$
   3) $^{77}_{34}Se$
   4) $^{78}_{36}Sc$

31. The number of electrons and neutrons of an element is 18 and 20 respectively. Its mass number is
   1) 2
   2) 17
   3) 37
   4) 38

32. The frequency of radiation emitted when the electron falls from $n=4$ to $n=1$ in a hydrogen atom will be (Given, ionisation energy of
   $103H=2.18 \times 10^{-18}$ J atom^{-1} and $h = 6.625 \times 10^{-34}$ Js)
   1) $1.54 \times 10^{15}s^{-1}$
   2) $1.03 \times 10^{15}s^{-1}$
   3) $3.08 \times 10^{15}s^{-1}$
   4) $2.00 \times 10^{15}s^{-1}$

33. Bohr model can explain
   1) The solar spectrum
   2) The spectrum of hydrogen molecule
   3) Spectrum of any atom or ion containing one electron only
   4) The spectrum of hydrogen atom only

34. Rutherford's experiment on the scattering of α −particles showed for the first time that the atom has
   1) Electrons
   2) Protons
   3) Nucleus
   4) Neutrons

35. The one electron species having ionisationenergy of 54.4 eV is
   1) H
   2) He^+
   3) B^{4+}
   4) Li^{2+}
   5) Be^{2+}

36. The wavelength of a spectral line emitted by hydrogen atom in the Lyman series is $\frac{16}{15R}$ cm. What is the value of n_2? (R=Rydberg constant)
   1) 2
   2) 3
   3) 4
   4) 1

37. The wave number of the spectral line in the emission spectrum of hydrogen will be equal to $\frac{8}{9}$ times the Rydberg's constant if the electron jumps from
   1) $n = 3$ to $n = 1$
   2) $n = 10$ to $n = 1$
   3) $n = 9$ to $n = 1$
   4) $n = 2$ to $n = 1$

38. The energy of hydrogen atom in its ground state is -13.6 eV. The energy of the level corresponding to the quantum number $n=5$ is
   1) -5.4 eV
   2) -0.54 Ev
   3) -2.72 eV
   4) -0.85 eV

39. According to Bohr's theory, the angular momentum of an electron in 5th orbit is
   1) $25\frac{h}{\pi}$
   2) $1.0\frac{h}{\pi}$
   3) $10\frac{h}{\pi}$
   4) $2.5\frac{h}{\pi}$

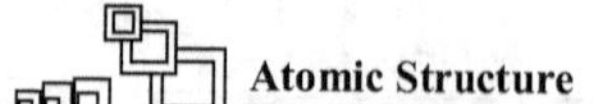

40. The number of photons emitted per second by a 60 W source of monochromatic light of wavelength 663 nm is ($h = 6.63 \times 10^{-34}$ Js)

   1) 4×10^{-20}
   2) 1.54×10^{20}
   3) 3×10^{-20}
   4) 2×10^{20}
   5) 1×10^{-20}

41. If the ionisation potential for hydrogen atom is 13.6 eV, then the ionisation potential for He^+ ion should be

   1) 13.6 eV
   2) 6.8 eV
   3) 54.4 eV
   4) 72.2 eV

42. Angular momentum of an electron in the n th orbit of hydrogen atom is given by

   1) $\dfrac{nh}{2\pi}$
   2) nh
   3) $\dfrac{2\pi}{nh}$
   4) $\dfrac{\pi}{2nh}$

43. The H-spectrum show

   1) Heisenberg's uncertainty principle
   2) Diffraction
   3) Polarisation
   4) Presence of quantised energy level

44. If the energy difference between the ground state of an atom and its excited state is 4.4×10^{-4} J, the wavelength of photon required to produce the transition

   1) 2.26×10^{-12} m
   2) 1.13×10^{-12} m
   3) 4.52×10^{-16} m
   4) 4.52×10^{-12} m

45. The H atom electron dropped from $n = 3$ to $n = 2$, then energy emitted is

   1) 1.9 eV
   2) 12 eV
   3) 10.2 eV
   4) 0.65 eV

46. Which transition in the hydrogen atomic spectrum will have the same wavelength as the transition, $n=4$ to $n=2$ of He^+ spectrum?

   1) $n = 4$ to $n = 3$
   2) $n = 3$ to $n = 2$
   3) $n = 4$ to $n = 2$
   4) $n = 3$ to $n = 1$
   5) $n = 2$ to $n = 1$

47. Bohr's radius of 2nd orbit of Be^{3+} is equal to that of

   1) 4th orbit of hydrogen
   2) 2nd orbit of He^+
   3) 3rd orbit of Li^{2+}
   4) First orbit of hydrogen

48. The energy of an electron in first Bohr orbit of H-atom is -13.6 eV. The possible energy value of electron in the excited state of Li^{2+} is

   1) -122.4 eV
   2) 30.6 eV
   3) -30.6 eV
   4) 13.6 eV

49. Energy of photon of visible light is

   1) 1 eV
   2) 1 MeV
   3) 1 eV
   4) 1 keV

50. Zeeman effect refers to the

   1) Splitting up of the lines in an emission spectrum in the presence of an external electrostatic field
   2) Random scattering of light by colloidal particles
   3) Splitting up of the lines in an emission spectrum in a magnetic field
   4) Emission of electrons from metals when light falls upon them

Single Correct Answer Type

1   **(2)**

Positron is as heavy as an electron.

2   **(1)**

The third alkaline metal is $^{40}_{20}\text{Ca}$. It contains 20 protons and 20 electrons.

3   **(2)**

$$\frac{e}{m} \text{ for electron}(e) = \frac{1.6 \times 10^{-19}}{9.1 \times 10^{-28}}$$
$$= 1.758 \times 10^{8}$$

$$\frac{e}{m} \text{ for proton}(p) = \frac{1.6 \times 10^{-19}}{1.672 \times 10^{-24}}$$
$$= 9.56 \times 10^{4}$$

$$\frac{e}{m} \text{ for neutron}(n) = \frac{0}{1.675 \times 10^{-24}} = 0$$

$$\frac{e}{m} \text{ for } \alpha - \text{particle} = \frac{2}{4} = 0.5$$

Hence, the increasing order of $\frac{e}{m}$ is as

$$n < \alpha < p < e$$

4   **(1)**

Rutherford showed the existence of nucleus in an atom by his α −particles scattering experiment. He postulated that every atom has a small central part which has positive charge and almost all the mass of atom ($i.e.$, nucleus consists of protons and neutrons).

5   **(2)**

A heavy element has atomic number X and mass number Y.

The atomic number of heavy element is smaller than its mass number.

$i.e.,$ $X < Y$

6   **(2)**

$N^{3-}\,7 + 3 = 10$ electrons

$F^{-}\,9 + 1 = 10$ electrons

$Na^{+}\,11 - 1 = 10$ electrons

7   **(2)**

J.J. Thomson (1987) was first experimentally demonstrated particle nature of electron. It was first of all proposed by Millikan's oil drop experiment.

8   **(4)**

Common name for proton and neutron is nucleon.

9   **(4)**

The isoelectronic species have same number of electrons.

1.   NaCl has Na^{+} and Cl^{-} ions

Electrons in $Na^+ = 11 - 1 = 10$

Electrons in $Cl^- = 17 + 1 = 18$

$\therefore$ They are not isoelectronic.

2.   CsF has Cs^+ and F^- ions

Electrons in $Cs^+ = 55 - 1 = 54$

Electrons in $F^- = 9+1=10$

$\therefore$ They are not isoelectronic.

3.   NaI has Na^+ and I^- ions

Electrons in $Na^+ = 11 - 1 = 10$

Electrons in $I^- = 53 + 1 = 54$

$\therefore$ These are not isoelectronic.

4. K_2S has K^+ and S^{2-} ions

Electrons in $K^+ = 19 - 1 = 18$

Electrons in $S^{2-} = 16 + 2 = 18$

$\therefore$ In K_2S, the ions K^+ and S^{2-} are isoelectronic.

10   **(2)**

$$e/m\text{ratio for }He^{2+} = \frac{2}{4}$$

$$e/m\text{ratio for }H^+ = \frac{1}{1}$$

$$e/m\text{ratio for }He^+ = \frac{1}{4}$$

$$e/m\text{ratio for }D^+ = \frac{1}{2}$$

$\therefore$ The e/m is highest for hydrogen.

11   **(3)**

Isotopes are atoms of same elements having different mass number

Isobars are atoms of different elements having same mass number.

Isotones are atoms of different elements having same number of neutrons.

Nuclear isomers are atoms with the same atomic number and same mass number but different radioactive properties.

11   **(3)**

Isotopes are atoms of same elements having different mass number

Isobars are atoms of different elements having same mass number.

Isotones are atoms of different elements having same number of neutrons.

Nuclear isomers are atoms with the same atomic number and same mass number but different radioactive properties.

12   **(1)**

No. of neutron=atomic mass−atomic number.

For C^{12} No. of neutron $= 12 - 6 = 6$

13   **(3)**

Nucleus of an atom is small in size but carries the entire mass $i.\,e.$, contains all the neutrons and protons.

14   **(3)**

Tritium contains 2 neutrons and 1 proton.

15   **(1)**

5.	J.J. Thomson	Determined charge on electron
6.	Neil Bohr	Gave structure of atom
7.	James Chadwick	Discovered neutron
8.	Mullikan	Carried out oil drop experiment

16   **(1)**

$_8O^{2-}$ has 10 electrons. $_{18}Ti^+$ has 80 electrons.

17   **(3)**

Isoelectronic species have same number of electron. Mg^{2+} and Na^+ both have 10 electrons hence, they are isoelectronic species.

18   **(3)**

Mass or proton $= 1.672614 \times 10^{27}$ kg

Mass of electron $= 1.60211 \times 10^{-31}$ kg

$\therefore$ Mass of proton/Mass of electron $= \dfrac{1}{1837}$

19   **(1)**

Isobars have same atomic mass but different atomic number.

Thus, the isobar of $_{20}Ca^{40}$ is $_{18}Ar^{40}$.

20   **(3)**

Number of electrons in $M^{2+} = 24$

$\therefore$ Number of electrons in $M = 26$

$i.e.$, atomic number $(Z)=26$

Mass number $(A)=56$

$\therefore$ Number of neutrons $=A - Z=56\text{-}26=30$

21 **(5)**

$^{14}_{6}C, ^{16}_{8}O, ^{15}_{7}N$ =isotonic triad

Isotonic=same number of neutron.

All species contain 8 neutrons.

22 **(2)**

Ar and Ca^{2+} are isoelectronic species as they have same number of electrons, $i.e.$, 18.

23 **(3)**

The proton has unit positive charge

$(+1.602 \times 10^{-19}C)$ and its mass is 1.007 u$(1.677 \times 10^{-27}kg)$.

24 **(3)**

Isotonic species are those species which have equal number of neutrons,

$e.g.$, $^{14}_{6}C, ^{15}_{7}N$ and $^{17}_{9}F$.

25 **(1)**

Isoeletronic means having same number of electrons. $K^{+}, Cl^{-}, Ca^{2+}, Sc^{3+}$ (all are having 18 electrons).

26 **(2)**

$Ca^{2+}(2, 8, 8)$ and Ar $(2, 8, 8)$ contains equal number (18) of electrons, hence they are isoelectronic.

27 **(3)**

When $n = 4$ and $x = 5$ then electronic configuration can be written as

$(4 - 1)s^2 (4 - 1)p^6 (4 - 1)d^5 4s^2$

This electronic configuration represents Mn and its atomic number is 25. Hence, number of protons are 25 in its nucleus.

28 **(3)**

Isotones are species which have equal number of neutrons.

Neutrons in $_{19}K^{39} = 39 - 19 = 20$

Neutrons in $_{20}Ca^{40} = 40 - 20 = 20$

29 **(1)**

Tritium is the isotope of hydrogen. Its composition is as follows :

1 electron, 1 proton and 2 neutrons

30 **(2)**

The isotones are a species which have equal number of neutrons.

No. of neutrons is $^{77}_{32}Ge = 77 - 32 = 45$

No. of neutrons in $^{77}_{33}As = 77 - 33 = 44$

No. of neutrons $\quad ^{77}_{34}Se = 77 - 34 = 43$

No. of neutron $\quad ^{77}_{36}Sc = 76 - 36 = 40$

No. of neutrons in $\quad ^{76}_{32}Ge = 76 - 32 = 44$

$\therefore \; ^{77}_{33}A$ is isotone of $\quad ^{76}_{32}Ge.$

31   **(4)**

The mass number =atomic number + number of neutron

Atomic number=no. of proton

$\qquad\qquad$ =no. of electron (for an atom)

So, mass number =18+20=38

31   **(4)**

The mass number =atomic number + number of neutron

Atomic number=no. of proton

$\qquad\qquad$ =no. of electron (for an atom)

So, mass number =18+20=38

32   **(3)**

Ionisation energy of H

$= 2.18 \times 10^{-18} J \, atom^{-1}$

$\therefore E_1$ (Energy of 1st orbit of H-atom)

$= -2.18 \times 10^{-18} J \, atom^{-1}$

$\therefore E_n = \dfrac{-2.18 \times 10^{-18}}{n^2} J \, atom^{-1}$

$Z = 1$ for $H - atom$

$\Delta E = E_4 - E_1$

$= \dfrac{-2.18 \times 10^{-18}}{4^2} - \dfrac{-2.18 \times 10^{-18}}{1^2}$

$= -2.18 \times 10^{-18} \times \left[\dfrac{1}{4^2} - \dfrac{1}{1^2} \right]$

$\Delta E = hv = -2.18 \times 10^{-18} \times -\dfrac{15}{16}$

$= +2.0437 \times 10^{-18} J \, atom^{-1}$

$\therefore \; v = \dfrac{\Delta E}{h} = \dfrac{2.0437 \times 10^{-18} J \, atom^{-1}}{6.625 \times 10^{-34} Js}$

$= 3.084 \times 10^{15} s^{-1} atom^{-1}$

33   **(3)**

Bohr's theory is applicable to unielectron atom or ion only.

34   **(3)**

Rutherford's scattering experiment for the first time showed the presence of positively charged nucleus at the centre of atom.

35   **(2)**

Out of other alternates, He^+ has ionisation energy of 54.4 eV because in He^+ effective nuclear charge is fairly high and ionic size is small.

36   **(3)**

For Lyman series,

$$\frac{1}{\lambda} = R\left[\frac{1}{1^2} - \frac{1}{n_2^2}\right]$$

$$\frac{15R}{16} = R\left[\frac{1}{1^2} - \frac{1}{n_2^2}\right]$$

$$\frac{15R}{16R} = \left[\frac{n_2^2 - 1}{n_2^2}\right]$$

$$\frac{15}{16} = \frac{n_2^2 - 1}{n_2^2}$$

$$15n_2^2 = 16n_2^2 - 16$$

$$n_2^2 = 16, n_2 = 4$$

37   **(1)**

Wave number of spectral line in emission spectrum of hydrogen,

$$\bar{v} = R_H\left(\frac{1}{n_1^2} - \frac{1}{n_2^2}\right) \qquad \ldots \text{(i)}$$

Given, $\bar{v} = \frac{8}{9}R_H$

On putting the value of $\bar{v}$ in Eq. (i), we get

$$\frac{8}{9} = R_H\left(\frac{1}{n_1^2} - \frac{1}{n_2^2}\right)$$

$$\frac{8}{9} = \frac{1}{(1)^2} - \frac{1}{n_2^2}$$

$$\frac{8}{9} - 1 = -\frac{1}{n_2^2}$$

$$\frac{1}{3} = \frac{1}{n_2}$$

$$\therefore \quad n_2 = 3$$

Hence, electron jumps from $n_2 = 3$ to $n_1 = 1$

38   **(2)**

Energy of e^- in the nth orbit of atom $= \frac{-13.6}{n^2}$ eV/atom

Given, $n = 5$

$$\therefore \quad E_5 = -\frac{13.6}{(5)^2} = -\frac{13.6}{25} = -0.54 \text{ eV/atom}$$

39 **(4)**

Angular momentum of an electron

$$= mvr = \frac{nh}{2\pi} \ (n \text{ is orbit number})$$

$$\text{in 5th orbit} = \frac{5h}{2\pi} = \frac{2.5h}{\pi}$$

40 **(4)**

$$\text{Energy}, E = \frac{nhc}{\lambda}$$

$$\Rightarrow 60 \times 1\text{Js} = \frac{n \times 6.63 \times 10^{-34}\text{Js} \times 3 \times 10^8 \text{m}}{663 \times 10^{-9}\text{m}} \left[\because \text{Power} = \frac{\text{energy}}{\text{time}}\right]$$

$$\therefore \quad n = \frac{60 \times 1 \times 663 \times 10^{-9}}{6.63 \times 10^{-34} \times 3 \times 10^8}$$

$$= 2 \times 10^{20}$$

41 **(3)**

IP for Fe^+ ion $=$ IP for $H \times (Z)^2$

where, $Z =$ atomic number

$$\therefore \text{IP} = 13.6 \times (2)^2$$

$$= 13.6 \times 4 = 54.4 \text{ eV}$$

42 **(1)**

According to Bohr, an electron can move only in those orbits in which its angular

momentum is a simple multiple of $\frac{h}{2\pi}$.

$i.e.,$ equal to $\frac{nh}{2\pi}$ (where, n is an integer)

43 **(4)**

Hydrogen spectrum is an emission spectrum. It shows the presence of quantized energy

levels in hydrogen atom.

44 **(4)**

$$\Delta E = h\nu = \frac{hc}{\lambda}$$

$$\lambda = \frac{hc}{\Delta E} = \frac{6.62 \times 10^{-34} \times 3 \times 10^8}{4.4 \times 10^{-14}}$$

$$= 4.52 \times 10^{-12}\text{m}$$

45 **(1)**

$$E_n = \frac{13.6}{n^2} \text{eV}$$

$$E_3 - E_2 = 13.6 \left(\frac{1}{(2)^2} - \frac{1}{(3)^2}\right) \text{eV}$$

$$E_3 - E_2 = 13.6 \left(\frac{1}{4} - \frac{1}{9}\right) \text{eV}$$

$$E_3 - E_2 = 13.6 \times \left(\frac{5}{36}\right) \text{eV}$$

$$= 1.9 \text{ eV}$$

46   **(5)**

$$\frac{1}{\lambda} = Z^2 , R_H \left[\frac{1}{n_1^2} - \frac{1}{n_2^2}\right]$$

For He$^+$, $\dfrac{1}{\lambda} = 2^2 . R_H \left[\dfrac{1}{2^2} - \dfrac{1}{4^2}\right] = 4 \times \dfrac{3}{16} = \dfrac{3}{4}$

For H, $\dfrac{1}{\lambda} = 1^2 . R_H \left[\dfrac{1}{1^2} - \dfrac{1}{2^2}\right] = \dfrac{3}{4}$

Hence, for hydrogen $n = 2$ ton $= 1$.

47   **(4)**

Bohr radius for nth orbit $= 0.53 \times \dfrac{n^2}{Z}$

Where, $Z =$atomic number

$\therefore$ Bohr radius of 2nd orbit of Be^{3+} $= \dfrac{0.53 \times (2)^3}{4}$

$$= 0.53 \text{ Å}$$

(d) Bohr radius of 1st orbit of H$= \dfrac{0.53 \times (1)^2}{1}$

Hence, Bohr's radius of 2nd orbit of Be^{3+}is equal to that of first orbit of hydrogen.

48   **(3)**

$$E_n = \frac{E_1}{n^2} \times Z^2$$

$$= \frac{-13.6}{4} \times 9 = -30.6 \text{ eV}$$

(for the excited state, $n = 2$ and for Li^{2+}ion, $Z = 3$)

49   **(1)**

$\lambda$for visible light is in the range of 400 to 780 nm.

$$E = \frac{hc}{\lambda}.$$

This, it is in the range of electron volt (eV).

50   **(3)**

Zeeman effect is splitting up of the lines of an emission spectrum in a magnetic field.